FIERCE COMPASSION

THE LIFE OF ABOLITIONIST DONALDINA CAMERON

*To Faith Presbyterian
God's best blessings
to you*

Kristin Wong

Kathryn Wong

Kristin and Kathryn Wong

Copyright © 2012 by Kristin Wong and Kathryn Wong
All rights reserved. No portion of this book may be reproduced in any manner without written permission, except for brief quotations in reviews or articles.

fiercecompassionbook.com

Published in Saline, Michigan by New Earth Enterprises
Cover design by Sarah Espinoza
Book design by Kathryn Wong

Front cover image courtesy of Department of Special Collections and University Archives, Stanford University Libraries

Back cover image courtesy of Janet Tang

All Scripture quotations, unless otherwise indicated, are taken from the Holy Bible, New International Version®, NIV®. Copyright ©1973, 1978, 1984 by Biblica, Inc.™ Used by permission of Zondervan. All rights reserved worldwide. www.zondervan.com

Scripture quotations marked (ESV) are from The Holy Bible, English Standard Version® (ESV®), copyright © 2001 by Crossway, a publishing ministry of Good News Publishers. Used by permission. All rights reserved.

ISBN: 978-0-9798318-2-9

Soli Deo Gloria

Table of Contents

Prologue *9*

Chapter One Kwai Ying *13*

Chapter Two Gold *21*

Chapter Three Growing Pains *29*

Chapter Four The Terror of Chinatown *39*

Chapter Five 920 for One Year *49*

Chapter Six Passing the Baton *61*

Chapter Seven Life and Death in a New Century *73*

Chapter Eight Of Love and Travel and the Like *85*

Chapter Nine Family Scrapbook *97*

Chapter Ten Though the Earth Give Way *107*

Chapter Eleven THE NEW 920 *117*

Chapter Twelve NATHANIEL *129*

Chapter Thirteen LOVE NEVER DIES *137*

Chapter Fourteen MAE AND MANION *147*

Chapter Fifteen ALLIES NEAR AND FAR *157*

Chapter Sixteen JUSTICE *169*

Chapter Seventeen THE ROSE OF PALO ALTO *179*

Chapter Eighteen SHE LIKES TO FLY AND BE FREE *187*

IS IT TRUE? *193*
CAMERON HOUSE TODAY *197*
SLAVERY TODAY *199*
TIMELINE *203*
WHO INSPIRED DONALDINA CAMERON? *206*
INDEX OF CHINESE CHARACTERS *209*
CHAPTER NOTES *210*
BIBLIOGRAPHY *217*
ACKNOWLEDGEMENTS *222*

Fierce Compassion

The Life of Abolitionist Donaldina Cameron

Prologue
920 Sacramento Street

Rusty-red bricks, uneven and lumpy, capture your attention as you walk up the hill on Sacramento Street. You stop in the shadow of the fortress-like building, five stories tall at the east end and three stories at the west. Pedestrians shuffle past you, down the hill to Chinatown or up to the Powell Street cable car. You notice a small plaque fastened onto the bricks, stating simply in English and Chinese, "Donaldina Cameron House, est. 1874."

Five steps bring you under the roof of a small, sheltering porch. You open the sturdy oak door, which is decorated with red grillwork and labeled with a gold-plated address: "920." After entering the building, you find yourself facing a dark wooden staircase. The sounds of Sacramento Street traffic recede as you walk up past three stained glass windows that cast pockets of colored light onto threadbare red carpet.

Near the second floor landing is an office, lined with filing cabinets and scattered with books, baskets, a large photograph of a youth group at summer camp. Strewn among coffee cups and computers lie brochures about counseling, tutoring, and domestic abuse. It seems a rather typical office of a busy social services agency. But scattered here and there are hints of something else, whispers of a deeply stirring history. There are stories in this place.

On a table in a corner sits a thick black book with a faded leather cover, fraying at the edge. You open it gingerly, trying not to damage the unraveling binding. It is a ledger book with heavy pages, faintly lined and filled with handwritten entries in black ink. The penmanship is elegant, though sometimes, it seems, its writer was rushed or fatigued. Each entry includes a name and a date, followed by a few details. Paging through the book awakens unanswered questions.

May 23/92. Si Foong. With the assistance of Officer Roy Clarkson and Ah Cheng as interpreter, we went to Ross Alley and rescued the aforementioned, a tall pleasant girl of perhaps 18 years of age.

December 6/92. Yoke Ying came alone to the home at noon. She is a young slave girl between thirteen and fourteen years of age—She learned she was to be sold to a life of shame and determined to make her escape—She is quite good looking and pleasant in appearance.

September 21/93. Little footed woman was brought here by the U.S. Customs officers to remain during the investigation to her right to land.

July 2/96. Ah Hah and Ah Seen. These two girls aged 8 and 5 years were brought to the home by doctor MG Woorley our physician. The parents live at 1117 and a half Stockton Street. The mother is sick and in debt having borrowed a good deal of money and the people to whom she is indebted threatened to sell the children.

Sometimes an entry ends with another date, weeks or months or years later, recording details of a departure: A ship passage to China.

A wedding. Death by typhoid. Or the lines might simply read, "Went away."

A few Western Union telegrams have been slipped into the black book, and a pressed rose, now papery-dry and faded. The pages go on and on. Names, dates, and cryptic stories, revealing only tantalizing hints of hope and discouragement, resilience and fragility, laughter and tears, and most of all, embedded in each handwritten line, fierce compassion and determined love.

This book holds a thousand stories. If only it could tell them all...

Chapter One
Kwai Ying

陷阱

He sits in ambush in the village;
in hiding places he murders the innocent.
His eyes stealthily watch for the helpless;
he lurks in ambush like a lion in his thicket;
he lurks that he may seize the poor;
he seizes the poor when he draws him into his net.
The helpless are crushed, sink down, and fall by his might.
Psalm 10:8-10 (ESV)

I remember the last time I saw the sun. My hands gripped the salt-soaked rail and I gazed back at Hong Kong as it shimmered in the heat. Aroma of wet wood, salt, and tar swirled together in the breeze that touched my cheek. I lifted my face to let warm beams engulf me, and then I squeezed through the opening and down into this dark cave. Now I sit in the dimness at the bottom of this ship, this monster ship with its strange foreign name: *President Cleveland*.

I am on my way to the Gold Mountain. When this long journey is over, I will work in a restaurant, far away from the dark filth of our room in the Hong Kong alley and far away from the bitter tongue of my mother, who curses my father every day for dying and leaving us nothing but debt. I am happy because I am brave enough to go on this voyage. I will save my family from shame.

I look at my tattered book, two hundred sheets of smudged paper tied together with string. These pages are full of details, so many details. They tell everything about the Li family and their village. If I wish to live in the land of the Gold Mountain, I must memorize every detail. I must convince the Americans that this is my family and my village, otherwise they will not let me in. To fail is to go back to Hong Kong. To go back to Hong Kong with empty hands is to destroy my mother. I have only one chance. I must remember everything. Everything. The names of each person in each house in the village. Where the rice is planted and which of my eight brothers and sisters goes to school. And the chickens, oh yes, the chickens. The number of chickens that live in the courtyard, who collects their eggs, who kills them on holidays. I study maps of the village and photographs of everyone in the Li family. I squeeze it all into my head.

Footsteps approach. The man who bought my passage to America and gave me the book sits next to me on the bunk. He coaches me each day, testing me with question after question. This is the man who came to my mother when it seemed sure we would starve completely and placed into her hands a thick wad of money. Her wide grin showed the gums where her teeth used to be. "I gave your mother some of your earnings in advance," he explained to me, "because I know that in America you will make so much money that you can easily pay me back." He is a good man and I call him Uncle.

Today, Uncle does not test me from the booklet. His countenance is solemn and he speaks in hushed tones. "In America, you desire to do well, to succeed and honor the name of your family. Listen to me. I must warn you. Dangers await you in America. When we arrive in San Francisco, one thing you must never, never do is go to the woman called Fahn Quai."

Fahn Quai: White Devil. A chill shudders down my spine. Uncle continues, "She lives in a large brick house on the top of a hill in Chinatown. They call it the mission house. Horrible things will happen if they catch you there. Fahn Quai keeps Chinese girls locked in the basement. She will torture you. She will poison you. The foreign devil women eat the organs of beautiful Chinese girls because they believe this will make them strong. Never go to the House on the Hill, little Kwai Ying."

There are many mysteries in America, things I do not understand. But I will listen and learn. I am full of good hope.

I am in America now. Early this morning, I took my small bag and joined the other weakened and bleary-eyed passengers as we stepped onto the deck. I was surprised by the brightness and the cold. My eyes adjusted to the dazzle of the sun, and I breathed the freshness of the air. I slipped to an empty spot along the rail and carefully dropped the book–my book full of lies about my identity–into the sea, so that the Americans will not catch me with it. It disappeared into the deep. Then I looked across the water and saw mountains rising above many strange, gray buildings. Elegant white birds soared up and up, gracefully catching the wind, so free. I have always loved birds. They fly to places I cannot go, and I am glad they welcome me here in this foreign land.

Then a startling and strange thing happened. While I watched the birds, a sailor approached me—a gigantic, pale-faced foreigner. My heart throbbed and fluttered in fear. The yellow-haired man stood next to me, leaned on the rail, and, like me, looked out to the mountains. Without turning towards me, he quietly spoke. I was astonished to hear his words come to me in Cantonese that I could understand. "If you ever need help, go to Kum Mai Lun. In English her name is Cameron. She lives at the mission home on the hill." And then, still without looking at me, he left.

Fierce Compassion

I am confused. Is this Kum Mai Lun the same as the white devil Fahn Quai? Does she eat Chinese girls, or does she help them? And why does the American sailor think that I would need help? Maybe later someone will explain this strange thing to me.

Yelling interrupted my thoughts. Sailors herded us off the ship. My legs wobbled as I walked down the gangplank. People waited on the dock, some Chinese and some foreigners. I recognized my "father" and "sister" from the photos in the book. I walked carefully toward them and gave a courteous bow and greeting. Then, American men in uniforms shouted in their strange language. A Chinese translator brought us to a building and into a huge room, shaped like a rectangle, with many gray chairs. Everything gray and cold, nothing at all like Hong Kong. Another American stood at the door, watching us.

The room held an anxious sort of silence, sometimes broken by a hum of hushed conversation. I did not see Uncle. I tried to remember what was on each page of the Li family book, starting at the beginning. I was only on page four when a man called my name, my new Li name, and one of the Americans brought me to a smaller room with bare, bright lights.

Three Americans sat behind a table, with a Chinese translator on the end. Two of the Americans took turns asking me questions while the other did something on a small machine; I think it was the typing machine that Uncle told me about. I had to name people in four photos, and they asked about my brothers and sisters, and the village school. But nothing about the chickens in the courtyard. I answered perfectly. Everything.

The man who had brought me to the room waited outside the door. When I was finished, he steered me out of the building into the cold air and to a line of people waiting behind a fence. I still did not see Uncle. I was sorry not to say goodbye to him. He was so kind to buy my passage to America and teach me how to live here. Soon I

Kwai Ying

spotted my "father" and "sister" again. They took me to a car and into the city...and oh, I cannot describe all the many new things I saw and heard.

My new father and sister seem to be cold and grim people. Now I am going to sleep and tomorrow—

❀

I have died and I am in hell.

❀

Occasionally through her delirious nightmare, Kwai Ying remembered what happened after those first hopeful moments in America. Her "father" and "sister" took her on a bewildering train trip from Seattle to San Francisco and then, flanking her on either side, they maneuvered through the streets of Chinatown. For a minute, the sun burst from behind misty fog, its rays warming her long, black hair. She rejoiced to hear the comfortable sounds of Cantonese, and was eager to reach the restaurant where she would prove herself as a waitress. Her two escorts brought her to a tenement on Jackson Street. The derelict structure with crooked, creaky stairs was not what Kwai Ying expected. A hard-faced woman opened the door. "This is another one of your sisters," her escort brusquely told Kwai Ying, "Wong So. Obey her."

Kwai Ying smiled and extended a traditional greeting, but Wong So only laughed bitterly. When the door closed, Wong So glanced at Kwai Ying with a mix of sympathy and petulance. Kwai Ying tried to understand. "I am here to be a waitress. Is this where I am to work?" Wong So remained silent.

The next morning, Kwai Ying was taken to a room in a hotel. She was told to undress. She was pushed onto an upturned wooden crate. Waves of realization, sickening realization, came over her, churning her stomach, even though she could barely grasp what was happening. Shadows from oil lamps made strange shapes on the walls. No rays of sun reached this place.

Men and women started entering from a door on the side of the room. They walked up and down, peering at other girls who stood on other crates. They reached Kwai Ying. Their eyes roved up and down her body and their hands grasped and prodded her skin. She flinched in anger. Her face took on a defiant expression. Prospective buyers balked at purchasing this one, for although she was beautiful and well-formed, she displayed too much spirit. Not enough subservience. She was the type that ran away.

But someone decided to take the risk. Kwai Ying recoiled when a middle-aged woman thrust several gold coins in her hand, a sham ceremony to prove that she was being paid to willingly sell her body. The coins were instantly grabbed back from her and she was shoved off of the crate.

Kwai Ying's whole body shook.

Nights were a kaleidoscope of colors and noise, harsh lights, and frightening darkness at hotels and clubs all around town. Men did to her as they pleased. Days were full of nightmarish memories that her mind could not escape. Waves of sickening anticipation of what would happen again in a few hours continually washed over her. Kwai Ying's good hope died. She was drowning in an ocean of pain.

Bill of Sale
Loo Wong to Loo Chee

April 16 - Rice, six mats, at $2...$12
April 18 - Shrimps, 50 lbs., at 10c................................$5
April 20 - Girl...$250
April 21 - Salt, fish, 60 lbs., at 10c...............................$6
$273

Received payment
Loo Chee
May 1, 1898

A sales receipt published in a San Francisco newspaper

Chapter Two
GOLD

淘金

God's providences are written in letters of gold across the months, dim sometimes through the mist of tears, but never quite hidden.
Donaldina Cameron

A crowd converged in the Utah wilderness. Two locomotives faced each other, one heading east, the other west. Around these brightly polished engines stood dapper political dignitaries, wealthy businessmen, engineers, railroad workers, and journalists. A band added to the patriotic festivity with each golden note that whirled in the gusty air. Politicians delivered victorious speeches. Men removed their hats for prayer. And then, all eyes turned to Mr. Leland Stanford, who grasped a silver-plated sledgehammer in his hefty hands and held it over a golden spike placed between the locomotives.

Up went the hammer, down came the hammer. No one knows whether it was Stanford's inexperience or merely a rush of adrenaline that made him miss his mark at first (much to his chagrin and the crowd's amusement), but finally the task was accomplished. Each hammer stroke was transmitted by telegraph to the east and west coasts, followed by the message: "Done." It was May 10, 1869, and the transcontinental railroad of the United States of America was complete.

Several Chinese men stood in the crowd. That evening, a few of them were invited to the luxurious dining car of railroad baron J.H. Strobridge, who knew that the ambitious enterprise of carving out this railroad, track by track, over and through the perilous Sierra Nevada mountains, could not have been accomplished without the gritty strength and perseverance of thousands of Chinese laborers.

Chinese men did not first come to America to build a great railroad. No, first they came for gold. Gold discovered at the site of Mr. Sutter's mill incited a mania that swept across continents. Fortune-seekers stampeded to California from South America, Europe, Asia, and Australia. Sailors abandoned their ships in San Francisco harbor and rushed to the mines.

Meanwhile, thousands of small villages in south China were staggering under disastrous weather and chaotic politics. Gangs of bandits exploited the country's turmoil and rampaged freely, stealing and killing. Families relinquished the last of their food, and then they starved.

News of gold traveled by ship from California to Hong Kong, then from person to person across muddy paths that connected the villages of south China. Shining stories of "Gum Shan"–the Golden Mountain–offered a glimmer of hope. Men bade farewell to their families, walked to Hong Kong, and bought passage to California, sometimes paid for by their entire clan. The survival of many a Chinese family came to rest on the gamble of the Gold Mountain.

In America's Wild West, courageous Chinese men played a harrowing game of survival. They lived on the outskirts of mining towns, scrounging for leftover gold at abandoned claims, or cooking and doing laundry for white miners. The Chinese were the scapegoats of mining society, often blamed when anything went wrong. Other miners taunted, threatened, robbed, and lynched them, sometimes cutting off their long braids as trophies. Before long, the Americans started churning out anti-Chinese laws. The California Supreme Court prohibited Chinese from testifying as witnesses against white citizens, rationalizing that the Chinese were "a race of people whom nature has marked as inferior, and who are incapable of progress or intellectual development beyond a certain point." Because the Chinese could not defend themselves in court, white miners harassed them without fear of consequences.

Leland Stanford, the silver-hammer-wielding railroad executive, was also a politician. Eight years before hammering the golden spike, Stanford had been elected governor of California. His inauguration speech added to the growing chorus of hostility toward the Chinese, as he insisted that "the settlement among us of an inferior race is to be discouraged, by every legitimate means...There can be no doubt but that the presence of numbers among us of a degraded and distinct people must exercise a deleterious influence upon the superior race." He promised to do everything he could to discourage Chinese immigration to the United States.

But Leland Stanford was also the president of the Central Pacific Railroad, one of the "Big Four" who pushed for the undertaking of a transcontinental railroad. He had a dilemma. After the first flush of excitement, the grand railroad looked like it might be derailed because there were not enough workers for the brutal, dangerous work of laying track. They needed an army of hardworking, skilled laborers. Instead, they were burdened with a few unreliable, unmotivated, unskilled men who would rather drink or disappear to the mines than tackle the strenuous work of railroad building. Progress was shoddy and slow. The railroad investors considered hiring children or Confederate prisoners from the recently ended Civil War. Then someone suggested Chinese workers. Skeptics contended that Chinese men were too small and stupid. But the bosses agreed to a trial, and were surprised to discover that the Chinese workers were accomplished, clever, and resilient. The railroad barons had found a "vast pool of cheap, plentiful, and easily exploitable labor." Leland Stanford, who had vowed to stop Chinese immigration, now sent recruiters to China to secure thousands of laborers.

The heckling and bullying endured by Chinese in the gold mines followed them to the railroad camps. Their pay was lower, and unlike other employees, they were expected to pay for their board; they brought their own tents had food carted in from San Francisco. During the peak of the most grueling work, Chinese laborers made up ninety percent of the Central Pacific's work force. With picks and dynamite, they carved tunnels through mountains and created narrow paths along the edge of precipices. Daily progress was sometimes measured in inches. Workers died of malnutrition and dynamite explosions. They froze or were buried in avalanches, their bodies discovered in the spring, sometimes with hands still grasping their picks.

As the glorious golden spike was plunged into the ground, celebrations from Boston and New York to Chicago and Denver toasted America's great ingenuity. And Chinese men who had survived the railroad packed their tents and meandered out of the Utah desert. Many returned to the city where their sojourn in the land of the Golden Mountain had begun: San Francisco.

Eleven weeks after Promontory Summit's golden spike, and more than 7,000 miles away, a mother gave birth to her seventh and last child. Allan and Isabella Cameron carefully wrote "Donaldina Mackenzie Cameron" in the family Bible next to the names of her five sisters and one brother. This baby's first home was a remote ranching outpost near the Scottish settlement of Dunedin, New Zealand, a pastoral land nestled between sea and mountains. Several years earlier, Allan and Isabella Cameron had packed their household and boarded a ship, leaving Scotland with four daughters and one son. They left their youngest daughter Isabella in their highland home to ease the pain of separation for grandparents. Then they ventured to the other end of the world in hopes of improving their fortunes in sheep ranching.

Two years after Donaldina's birth, the Camerons decided to transplant themselves again. This time they set out for the United States of America, where there was rumor of a different kind of gold: undulating fields of ranching pasture. Allan went ahead to scout out the land, then sent for his wife and six children to follow. Isabella Cameron embarked on a long voyage: six months with six children, including Donaldina, her affectionate, hazel-eyed toddler, called Dolly.

Finally, the ship from New Zealand floated through the narrow strait that connects the Pacific Ocean with San Francisco Bay. Dolly Cameron clapped with delight, watching with her sisters and brother as San Francisco emerged from the moist haze. The ship docked at one of the bustling wharves of the burgeoning pioneer city. From the safety of her mother's arms, little Dolly laughed. None of the family knew that just a stone's throw away were other girls, surreptitiously tucked away on neighboring ships, who would soon be slipped to auction rooms and sold as slaves.

San Francisco's hillsides were filling with new hotels, restaurants, parks, churches, libraries, and opera houses. A fellow passenger recommended the American Exchange Hotel on Sansome Street as a good place for Mrs. Cameron to wait for her husband. So mother and children, shaky on their sea legs, collected their trunks, secured a carriage, and headed into San Francisco.

The next morning, little Dolly stood with her nose flattened against the hotel window, watching the rainy street below. The hotel overlooked Chinatown, and Dolly's eyes were fixed on a stream of Chinese men on their way to work at a cigar factory. They wore loose trousers and held black umbrellas, and long braids lay on their backs. Dolly's sisters and brother soon lost interest. But Dolly was mesmerized.

Fierce Compassion

If Scottish gentlewoman Isabella Cameron had any inkling of the perils that her little daughter would later plunge into on these Chinatown streets, she would have been astonished. But the shock might have been mixed with pride. The enthusiastic Cameron and Mackenzie families had a history of zealous audacity. Years later, when people marveled at the intrepid courage of Donaldina Cameron, who plucked slave girls right out of the hands of their owners, she quipped that her vocation for slave-rescuing mission work came straight from the legacy of her Scottish ancestors: a combination of devout Presbyterian clergymen and border-raiding sheep rustlers.

Gold in the mines, gold in a railroad spike, and gold in the promise of an auburn-haired Scottish girl carried in her mother's arms from New Zealand to California. Many people from many nations fixed their hopes on the land that the Chinese called Gold Mountain. On one side of the railroad's famous gold spike, a prayer was engraved: "May God continue the unity of our Country, as this Railroad unites the two great Oceans of the world." While important men dreamed of the greatness of a growing nation, a little girl gazed out a window at Chinese men walking in the rain.

This photo by Arnold Genthe, titled "The Street of the Gamblers by Day" is a striking image of the many men and few women who lived in San Francisco's Chinatown.

Chapter Three
Growing Pains

成長

*The Lord is close to the brokenhearted
and saves those who are crushed in spirit.*
Psalm 34:18

Dolly thrived on her family's quintessentially western sheep ranch in the San Joaquin Valley. She scampered over rolling hills, frolicked in fields of wildflowers, and soaked up the affectionate doting of her parents and older siblings. For the mother of the clan, however, pioneer life was taxing. The house was hot in summer and cold in winter. It was hard to bring food out of the ground and keep dust out of the house, and she was raising six children in a remote ranch far from the support of extended family. When an infamous group of bandits rode their horses up to the house one day and demanded whiskey, it was exciting for the children, but harrowing for their mother. This rigorous life exacted a costly toll.

One spring morning, five-year-old Dolly awoke to sunlight pouring in through the wispy white curtains of the bedroom she shared with her sisters. She smiled, basking in the warmth, but then her smile faded. She was an intuitive girl, and she felt tension pulling their home like a subtle but strong current. Why had she been allowed to sleep so late? Her mother had been sick, but today she was going to be better, so that they could go together to the meadow where the baby blue eyes were blooming.

The house was eerily silent. She opened the door and tiptoed outside to the bench under the cottonwood tree. Her brother, Allan, sat, head in his hands. "Allan!" Dolly blurted out, relieved to find someone. "What's wrong?" Dolly had never seen her stalwart older brother crying.

"Mama's not better, Dolly. Now go away."

"But she told me that she would be all better today and she said she would go to the field with me to pick flowers. She told me that she would be all better today, Allan!" Dolly's eyes widened with fear.

When Donaldina turned to run into the house, her father appeared in the door, scooped her up, and carried her inside. "Mama won't be picking flowers with you today, Dolly."

Dolly's lips began to tremble, "But she told me that–"

"I'm sorry Dolly. Mama's too sick. She's more sick than she was yesterday, and I don't think she's going to get better this time. You can still see her, though. She said goodbye to everyone else; now she'd like to say goodbye to you."

A few hours later, Dolly sat in the field of flowers all by herself. "Mama?" she whispered, "Won't you come and pick blue eyes with me?" But the only response was the wailing wind and far off cry of a hawk: piercing, harsh, desolate. She gathered the handful of flowers she had picked all by herself and started walking home.

After their mother's death, the older children took more responsibility. Each night, they gathered around the fire and listened to their father read Scripture, and sometimes Charles Dickens or Sir Walter Scott. They sang together, too, and the cadence and diction of psalms, hymns, and British literature worked their way into the rhythms of Dolly's Scottish lilt, bestowing her with an eloquence that she would

Growing Pains

use to speak for others all of her life. The family often declared that Donaldina had inherited her mother's charm and gentility.

Despite the loss of their mother and wife, the Camerons persevered. They accrued wealth as their flocks multiplied. But many threats loomed over western ranchers. One cold, rainy night, Dolly's father went out to check the sheep and did not stagger back through the door until the first hint of dawn was touching the sky. When his children saw him, bedraggled and spattered with sheep blood, they led him to the chair by the fire. In broken sentences, he relayed the story. Sheep rustlers. He spotted them in the distance, through the rain, slinking away with his sheep. He gave chase, gaining on them, and then they saw him. He watched helplessly as the men deliberately, maliciously slit the sheep's throats and heaved them into the river. He spent the rest of the night searching for the few straggling sheep who had escaped.

Donaldina Cameron as a girl

The ranch could not recover from such a blow. The Camerons moved away from the rolling hills and fresh air into the city of San Jose, and then to Oakland, where Allan Cameron could find work on other people's farms.

"The Chinese must go!" In the summer of 1877, the streets around San Francisco City Hall clamored with resentful shouting. The crowd swelled to thousands, encouraged in its frenzy by Irish immigrant Dennis Kearney, who accused the Chinese of stealing American jobs. Agitated men moved toward Chinatown, grabbing bricks and stones, smashing the windows of any building that looked Chinese. They broke into a grocery store, taking the liquor, then set fire to a Chinese tenement. Some headed for the wharves, to the ships that brought the Chinese to America, and burned down their lumberyards. Anti-Chinese riots threatened to endanger the whole city, and the San Francisco police recruited a five thousand man vigilante army to prevent disaster.

European-Americans had been happy to let the Chinese work at dirty, backbreaking, low-paying jobs in mining towns and on the railroad when better opportunities abounded. But when unemployment rose, so did hostility toward these foreigners. They spoke Chinese instead of learning English. They dressed and ate differently. They were Buddhists. They did not fit in. The Chinese, meanwhile, thought of America as an uncultured, barbaric wasteland, and most never intended to settle permanently, so their motivation to assimilate into American culture was low. The longer they did not conform, the more the Americans resented them. All along the west coast, hatred toward the Chinese festered. Congressmen wrote laws to harass them. Newspapers printed degrading articles about them. Sneering boys ambushed them in the streets.

Anti-Chinese fervor spread across the country. Congress passed its first restrictive federal immigration law, the Page Act, which prevented the entry of "undesirable" immigrants in order to "end the danger of cheap Chinese labor and immoral Chinese women." Then Congress slammed the door on practically all Chinese immigration with the Chinese Exclusion Act. Diplomats, merchants, and students could enter, but others were shut out, and Chinese already living in the United States could not own property or become citizens, nor could their children attend public schools. No other ethnicity was singled out so pointedly in immigration policy. Racism was legalized.

Instead of helping Chinese conform to American culture, the

Exclusion Act forced them to live a life apart. Instead of encouraging Chinese to comply with American law, it challenged them to a battle of wits with immigration officials whose job it was to keep them out of the country. Instead of ending Chinese prostitution, it created an environment that increased the demand for women and encouraged illegal, brutal slave traffic.

By the time the Exclusion Act was passed in 1882, more than 70,000 Chinese were living in San Francisco, crowded into Chinatown's twelve blocks, where upper stories were haphazardly added onto wooden tenements that jutted out over the streets. It was a shocking change from the lush green rice paddies of the Pearl River Valley to the urban landscape of San Francisco's Chinatown. Strangers shared quarters, sleeping in shifts, three to a bed. The men worked long, hard hours at menial jobs, often "women's work" that would have disgraced them in China. Anytime they stepped outside Chinatown they were likely to be heckled and physically attacked. They were lonely and homesick.

Very few married Chinese men could legally bring their wives from China, nor were most single men allowed to bring brides. It was also illegal for Chinese immigrants to marry Americans. Thus, tens of thousands of young Chinese men living in America were forbidden to marry. By 1880, in a terribly imbalanced society, there were twenty men living in San Francisco's Chinatown for each woman.

To stay in America meant living with heckling, hard work, low pay, and loneliness. But to return to China often meant financial ruin for their families.

Canton did not have enough food. California did not have enough women. Clever entrepreneurs turned girls and women into merchandise. An organized slave market began to thrive. The merchants in this business of human smuggling bought daughters from desperate parents, or lured teenagers with promises of lucrative jobs or wealthy husbands, or abducted those who would not come willingly. Some of this human merchandise was sold to rich Chinese settlers

Fierce Compassion

looking for domestic slaves, second wives, or concubines. The rest of the girls and women were forced to sign contracts that they could not read, selling themselves into prostitution.

Fourteen was considered the ideal age for a prostitute. The prettiest ones were sent to exotic parlor houses where they were dressed in silk, powdered with makeup, scented with perfume, and trained to smile, flirt, sing and do anything that Chinese and Anglo-American clients demanded. The rest landed at the bottom of the pile, the dreadful "cribs," which were tucked into Chinatown's narrow, dimly lit alleys. Girls shared twelve-foot long stalls, taking turns at the grated windows, where they called out to attract the attention of passing men and boys. Crib prostitutes were harshly treated by their owners and customers, closely guarded, and severely punished. Once a week, they were secured with dog leashes and paraded through Chinatown on display. When they became worn out or diseased, they were discarded on the street or stored in a room to die alone.

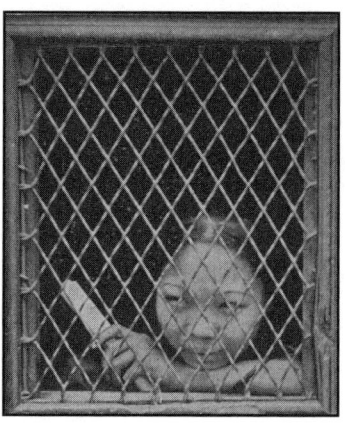

A Chinese slave peers out of her crib in San Francisco's Chinatown, 1905.

The system allowed a sliver of possibility for eventual release, but "most Chinese prostitutes were subjected to such physical and mental abuse that few could outlive their contract terms."

The Chinese in California had few American friends. But they did have a few. A few devout Christians, propelled by their faith, dedicated their lives to seeking the well-being of the Chinese. At the height of anti-Chinese hysteria, several pastors and their wives–

Growing Pains

notably from Presbyterian, Congregational, Methodist, and Baptist denominations–befriended San Francisco's Chinese residents. They started to know them as individuals instead of generalizations. These pastors pointed out the hypocrisy and selfishness of Chinese racism and spoke strongly against the harsh and exploitative treatment the Chinese suffered. To advocate for Chinese immigrants, the Methodist Reverend Otis Gibson spoke courageously and wrote insistently in the local press and other venues. During one day of anti-Chinese violence, Gibson stood outside to try to prevent the burning of a Chinese business. Rioters pelted him with stones.

The Presbyterian Reverend Augustus Loomis told of the misery of teenagers and women who were bought and sold, beaten, raped, abused, and left to die just a few blocks from the comfortable homes of those in his church. Some in his congregation caught his fervor. Several women gathered with Mrs. Loomis and Mrs. Conduit, the wife of another pastor, to talk more about this horrifying slavery and what they might do about it. Perhaps inspired by the new Methodist work for Chinese women, they dreamed up a plan to establish a safe house for women in Chinatown.

On the afternoon of September 1, 1874, the same year that the Cameron children said goodbye to their mother, a quiet dedication ceremony took place in San Francisco's Chinatown. A small coterie of respectable Victorian women, with their sweeping dresses and ribboned hats, gathered quietly in a small apartment that looked out on the bustle of Jackson Road. Several Chinese friends joined them. This new apartment was to be set apart as a refuge for Chinese women and girls, with hopes that some who were suffering would hear about the home and find ways to flee to it. If any slaves did make it to the home, these devout and earnest Presbyterian women intended to offer them housing, healing, education, respect and love.

The small group admiring the apartment that afternoon could not possibly have imagined the significance of what was beginning.

Fierce Compassion

The prayer of dedication given by Reverend Loomis was a small pebble dropped into a large lake, seemingly swallowed by deep water, but starting a ripple that would keep moving out and out.

A newspaper celebrates the signing of the Chinese Exclusion Act

Chapter Four
The Terror of Chinatown

恐懼

It is a humiliating fact that the greatest enthusiasm is often manifested upon issues where ignorance, bigotry, prejudice and selfishness play the principal parts.
Reverend Otis Gibson

Miss Houseworth and Miss Worley clambered down the steps of the Mission Home. Umbrellas offered spotty protection from the frigid January rain that pelted them as they progressed east on Sacramento Street to the herbal shop, where several police from the Chinatown squadron waited. Together the group turned onto Jackson Street, where odors of trash and smoke penetrated the cold, damp air. Miss Houseworth gestured furtively at a foreboding door, bolted with iron and plastered with soggy paper covered in Chinese characters. This door would certainly not open to their knock, so one of the police officers entered the neighboring restaurant, climbed up the back stairs, heaved himself onto the roof and broke into the intended destination through a skylight. He unbolted the door and motioned the others inside.

They climbed up rickety, dark stairs to the room where they hoped to find a ten-year old girl. The room was empty. They knocked on another door and searched in another vacant tenement and another, and another, until on the seventh attempt they discovered a woman glowering over a small girl whose face and arms were covered with burns and bruises. Ignoring the woman's protests, a police officer gently scooped up the whimpering child and carried her down the stairs and out the door. Back they walked through the rain to the Mission Home. Older girls encircled the new arrival, eager to cover her with dry clothes and warm sympathy. Later that night, the home's director, Miss Margaret Culbertson, sat at her desk to write in the thick black ledger:

> *January 17/94. Teen Fook was rescued by Miss Houseworth, Miss Florence Worley and some police officers from her inhuman mistress who lived on Jackson St. near Stockton St. The child had been very cruelly treated—her flesh pinched and twisted till her face was scarred. Another method of torture was to dip lighted candlewicking in oil and burn her arms with it. Teen Fook is a pretty child of about ten years old, rosy cheeked and fair complexion.*

Before her life as a household slave, Teen Fook, later called Tien Wu, had lived with her family in a southern Chinese village. One morning when she was five years old, Tien Wu was particularly excited about a visit to her grandmother. Her face glowed with repeated cleanings, and her clothes were neatly folded and packed away. Tien Wu did not understand why her mother choked and sobbed when saying goodbye. "Don't cry, Mama," said the little girl. "I'm just going to see Grandma and then I will be right back." Tien Wu was a little afraid of her father, who was waiting, distantly dispassionate, by the door. Young as she was, she understood that the reason she sometimes went to bed with no food in her belly was that her father gambled away all his pennies. She did not understand what "debt" meant, but she knew it was a bad word that was somehow connected with her father and her hunger.

The Terror of Chinatown

Tien Wu followed her father through the village and beyond. She smelled the sea before she saw it, surprised because she did not remember this salty tang in the air by her grandmother's house. Her father led her right up to the water, onto a ferry and into a small room, where he left her, locking the door behind him. She never saw him again.

In the next bewildering days, Tien Wu was transferred from the small ferry to a large ship. The voyage etched itself deeply into her memory–the mechanical churning noises, the stench of the hold, the strange faces of people who looked nothing like those from her village. She was haunted by the memory of her mother's despairing sobs. Little Tien Wu landed in San Francisco and was sold as a child household slave. She spent long days cooking and cleaning, her owner's baby strapped to her back. When she faltered, her face was pinched or her arms burned with candles.

Enticing flyers plastered around Hong Kong promised that Gold Mountain adventurers would discover "great pay, large houses, and food and clothing of the finest description." But a Chinese-English phrasebook of the time hinted at another reality. It taught its readers sentences useful for life in America:

I cannot trust you.
He took it from me by violence.
They were lying in ambush.
He was murdered by a thief.
He committed suicide.
He was choked to death with a lasso by a robber.
He was starved to death in prison.
He was going to drown himself in the bay.
He tried to assassinate me.
He was smothered in his room.
He was shot dead by his enemy.

Chinatown alley with prostitute "cribs"

The Gold Mountain was not safe. To survive this hostile country, Chinese settlers banded together in civic associations, organized by family clan and county of origin, which helped immigrants in their new home. Men arriving in America joined one of these organizations as quickly as possible. A few immigrants found themselves outside the protection of these groups; they lacked clan ties, perhaps, or had been expelled by their associations, and so they formed their own alternative affiliations. Some of these developed into organized crime gangs which became skillful at extracting money from their countrymen. Taking advantage of the misery of displaced, lonely men, they started amassing fortunes from opium, gambling, and prostitution.

The West Coast media, when its attention was captured by the presence of these criminal organizations, misinterpreted the Cantonese word "tong," which means "association," and applied it narrowly to groups of malevolent Chinese gangs, when in fact most of the tongs were altruistic social service associations. Due to this misuse of "tong" by sensationalistic writers in the late 19th century, Americans started to associate the word with criminal gangs. (Although its original mild connotation has taken on a more sinister meaning, we will keep the historical precedent and use "tong" to refer to crime organizations.)

The tongs built alliances. San Francisco police and politicians pocketed gifts of cash and jewels and then kept quiet while crimes were committed. The tongs employed assassins, nicknamed hatchetmen, who carried out murders during feuds between rival groups. Hatchetmen also intimidated or killed anyone who neglected to pay protection money, refused to lie to authorities about slave girls, or went to school to learn English. A man targeted by a tong might see his name ominously posted on a wall along a Chinatown street as warning that he was marked for violent death. Police officer Michael Smith stated grimly of the gangs, "They are the terror of Chinatown."

After work in mines and railroads ran out, Chinese men wended their way from remote camps back to West Coast cities, especially San Francisco. Before the Gold Rush, San Francisco had been a ramshackle fishing town. Twenty years later, it was "tall, handsome, dignified. Muddy wagon trails had given way to paved streets…along them rose stately buildings of stone and brick, designed in Goth, Italian, and other classical architectural styles."

But Chinese men found California more barbaric than civilized. Americans resented the Chinese, who accepted low pay and squalid work, and then the immigrants discovered that newly formed tongs

Fierce Compassion

were also eager to exploit them. These harassed men found themselves threatened both by Americans and their own countrymen, "ground between the hoodlums and bigots on one side and their own criminals and tong bullies on the other."

Most Chinese immigrants were peaceful and law-abiding, working hard to send every penny they could spare to their families in China. But the activities of the few illicit tongs became an excuse for the virulent anti-Chinese prejudice of many Americans. San Francisco newspapers warned of the moral and physical dangers that threatened white families because of Chinese immigration. Readers shook their heads and turned away, clucking their tongues at the depravity of the Chinese race.

Meanwhile, whispers started slipping through the doors of Chinatown brothels: some white American women were inviting any slaves who could escape to a refuge on Prospect Street. The lives of these sex slaves were often so horrendous that they tried to end their shame and torture through suicide. Now there was rumor of a possible alternative. Less than three weeks after the dedication of the Presbyterian mission apartment, the brand new ledger book recorded its first resident, 24-year-old Ah Woo, who had been brought to America two years earlier and sold into prostitution. Shortly afterwards came 16-year-old Jin Ti, whose gambling father had sold her as a domestic slave years earlier. The time was approaching when she would be forced into prostitution: she fled first, and after two years in the home was happily married to a Christian young man.

Those first runaways were courageous. They did not know what might happen to them at this foreigners' home. And they trembled with the certainty that if they were caught on the way they would risk a beating, or worse, and that any prostitution contracts that allowed a sliver of a possibility of eventual release would be changed to condemn them to spend the rest of their lives under the yoke of slavery. Utter desolation pushed them to risk everything.

The Terror of Chinatown

After those first two young women made it safely to the mission, others followed. The women at the home offered the runaways protection and helped them with gradual healing from disease and abuse. Just as the founders had envisioned, the slave survivors received food, clothing, education, protection, and an introduction to a God who loved them. Previously sheltered, respectable women of Victorian San Francisco nursed the venereal sores of teenagers and dedicated themselves to the humbling, hard work of building trust and crossing cultures. Sometimes the girls met sympathy with suspicion, but the real love of the mission house community eventually won most of them over. (It also helped when the missionaries decided to serve Chinese food rather than American, and replaced coffee with tea!)

This safe house was not popular with Americans or Chinese. A police escort had to be secured when the mission home ventured out to Sunday worship: the women were in danger of assault from agitated Americans who blamed the Chinese for their problems, and in danger of kidnapping by infuriated Chinese slave-owners who wanted their property back. But while press, politicians, and public ranted anti-Chinese slogans, these courageous women kept building their household of outcasts. They raised money. They taught classes. They invited girls to their homes. They planned special events to add sweetness to the hard work of building a new life after abuse.

After two years, the mission had outgrown its small apartment and needed more spacious living quarters. But Americans were not inclined to donate to a mission for immoral Chinese women, and Chinese were apprehensive about Americans living in their territory. The mission's leaders were treated with contempt. Once, when a board member visited a home in Chinatown to ask about rental, the landlord spat in her face.

They eventually found new lodging. The work continued to thrive, and soon the second home also overflowed. It had been intended to house fifteen girls; by the time that small Tien Wu arrived, there were forty residents, sleeping three to a bed. By then, the Presbyterian women had been speaking zealously about their work for twenty years to anyone who would listen. Their enthusiastic perseverance had begun to permeate the hard ground of racism. Contributions came from around the country until there was enough to build a new home.

It was dedication day. Friends and guests mingled with mission house staff and residents outside the new brick building on 920 Sacramento Street, at the western edge of Chinatown. They gazed west for a glimpse of the famous Nob Hill mansions, then turned around and saw Chinatown spread below them, with the ferry building and San Francisco Bay beyond. T'sang T'sun, one of the home's first slave survivors, had been chosen to lay the symbolic cornerstone. When T'sang T'sun was a young girl in China, she had been sold to a man who shaved her head and dressed her in boys' clothing so that she could pass as his son. Several years later, she heard that she was about to be sold again, this time into prostitution. She had heard rumors about the foreigners' mission, and there she ran. Now, she set down the hopeful cornerstone of her new home, carefully proclaiming, "With strong faith in the salvation of my countrywomen in this land and in China, I lay this cornerstone in the name of Jesus Christ." Those gathered around her smiled, while tense tong leaders surreptitiously observed the celebration of this irritating enterprise.

The adventures of the home fondly dubbed "920" were about to begin.

"Allan! Come down to the creek! It's the Fourth of July. Eleanor and I need you to help us be Washington crossing the Delaware." The gallant brother obliged his youngest sister Dolly and her friend. After the girls rocked, tipped, and capsized the boat, he dragged them to safety and helped them creep stealthily into the house to avoid Annie's disapproval of their stained white dresses.

Older sister Annie served as Dolly's mother in many ways, and her other siblings bestowed her with other enduring gifts. Katherine delighted in telling dramatic stories from literature and the Scottish highlands, and Helen loved to talk about the Bible, showing her little sister how to recognize the presence of God all around. To her family, Dolly was the adored baby sister, fun-loving, charming, and always effusively compassionate toward anyone who needed comfort or help.

Dolly Cameron met Eleanor Olney and Evelyn Browne when the Camerons moved to Oakland, and the three of them soon became a dynamic trio, forged into friendships that would remain for the duration of their lives. It also happened that Evelyn's mother, Mrs. P.D. Browne, was president of the board that was responsible for the ambitious undertakings of the Chinatown Presbyterian mission home. While Mrs. Browne energetically served a growing household of slave survivors, her daughter Evelyn romped about with the energetic Camerons.

When their father was offered a job managing a ranch in southern California, the Cameron family moved again. They invited new friends into their vibrant circle and kept up with their Oakland friends as well. Once, when the Browne family was visiting the Camerons, Evelyn couldn't find the chum she affectionately called "Donald." Then she spotted her friend perched perilously on the platform of the windmill, auburn hair flying wildly in the wind as she attempted a repair. Rather alarmed, Evelyn brought her father to the window. Mr. Browne, knowing Dolly's spunk, chuckled, "I guess she will take care of the situation all right." Soon the windmill was as good as new and "Donald" was safely back on the ground.

After her high school graduation, Donaldina enrolled in a teacher-training program in Los Angeles. While she was in her first year there, grief struck the Camerons again: their father died. Donaldina left college and moved back to the ranch with her brother and unmarried sisters. She helped manage the home. And she enjoyed the company of her brother's friend George. One month before her nineteenth birthday, Dolly shared her romance in a letter written to her sister Jessie (nicknamed Jacko), who was married and living in Hawaii:

> *My darling sister, how shall I begin to tell you what joy it gave me that you were so cordial about George's and my engagement. You would be glad if you only knew how very happy your dear letter made me. I would have written myself and told you, but George loves so to handle his pen and seemed eager to write so I let him. I am awfully glad that you feel warmly to him Jacko for I would hate to marry anyone that some of my family didn't like…Just think if George should happen to have enough money by the time we're married to take a trip to the Islands…*

Dolly was engaged. But she did not marry George, and the reason remains a mystery. In later years she calmly refused to speak about the topic. We do know that by the age of nineteen, Donaldina Mackenzie Cameron had lost both parents, dropped out of college, and suffered a broken engagement.

Chapter Five
For One Year

憐憫

The cords of death entangled me; the torrents of destruction overwhelmed me.
The cords of the grave coiled around me; the snares of death confronted me.
In my distress I called to the Lord; I cried to my God for help.
From his temple he heard my voice; my cry came before him, into his ears.
Psalm 18:4-7

Sycamore leaves cast dappled shadows on the parlor floor as Donaldina rushed about in an excited bustle, preparing for guests. She cracked open the windows to invite a breeze, peering out to watch for the arrival of her friends. She tripped around the room buoyantly, her cream-colored dress accentuating her fine complexion and her tumbling mass of thick curls restrained by a lace cap that sat above her dark brows. Six years had passed since Donaldina's father died and her engagement ended, six years since she had dropped out of college to help her brother and sisters on the ranch. A visit from Mrs. Browne and Evelyn was a happy holiday.

The visitors arrived, and the Cameron porch hummed with sounds of affectionate exclamations and embraces. Later that afternoon, a merry party of three—Donaldina, Evelyn, and Mrs. Browne—took the buggy out for a ride on the country roads. Mrs. Browne kept her hand on the reins, and as they meandered past fields and trees she talked to Donaldina about the Mission House in San Francisco's Chinatown. Donaldina listened with spellbound attention to stories of clandestine midnight slave rescues, her imagination ignited by Mrs. Browne's description of sinister Chinese crime, contemptuous American prejudice, and the Chinese and American women who had set out to overcome both.

Mrs. Browne adjusted her elegant spectacles in a characteristic sweep of the hand. "And so Miss Culbertson has developed ingenious and daring ways to outwit these criminals and rescue their slave girls. And then, oh you should see what happens to these forlorn little fugitives when they are given help and sympathy, with a Christian education, wholesome recreation, and practical skills. Light dawns for the first time on those deep valleys of sickness and shame.

"The work that Miss Culbertson does is truly remarkable, Dolly, wonderful indeed. She is fighting valiantly to overcome one of this country's social and moral calamities. And yet," Mrs. Browne hesitated briefly before continuing, "and yet, I have begun to feel as of late that a reprieve would do her an abundance of good. The need is so overwhelming, and Miss Culbertson is becoming frail from the strain of the work. She needs an assistant, someone with fresh energy to help carry the burdens." There was a short pause in the conversation; the clopping of horse hooves on the gravel road was the only sound.

Quite abruptly, Mrs. Browne pulled the buggy to a stop in the shade of a large roadside tree.

"Donaldina Mackenzie Cameron, don't you want to do something?"

Donaldina's face revealed mingled astonishment and questioning excitement. "Me!" she managed to gasp. "Why, I'm not qualified in the least. I am not–"

"Nonsense," interrupted the older woman, "You are more than qualified. Won't you please just consider it? You could teach the sewing and I am sure you would be a help to Miss Culbertson in other ways as well. Not to mention all that your love and vitality could bring to those girls. Dolly, I believe that if your deep gladness met the world's deep need, it would make a tremendous difference. Just for a year, Dolly. Pray on it a little while, but in the end, take me up on my proposal, of course! I think that you might be exactly what our home needs."

Mrs. Browne's intuition was perfect. Donaldina Cameron had a grand sense of fun and humor, and her personality and speech were full of charm, but she could also act with steely courage. Her devoted family had given her confidence and strength. Her naturally compassionate temperament had been deepened by grief and loss. And she had a rooted and robust faith in God. Donaldina was prepared for long days of teaching and long nights of nursing. She would be able to steadfastly face corruption, hostility, legal battles, financial struggles, and death threats, as well as plague, earthquake, and fire. Though this Scottish-blooded, New Zealand-born, California-raised young woman did not yet know it, she was poised to take on "the terror of Chinatown."

Donaldina looked out that night on a starry sky. She had made up her mind to say yes to Mrs. Browne's proposal. She would go to Chinatown. For a year.

The young gentlewoman stepped off the train and onto the burgeoning San Francisco street, her calm exterior belying the adventurous sparkle in her eyes. Her auburn hair was piled on her head and topped by a hat, with a loose veil that framed her face. The frills of her blouse lightened the dark gray jacket, and her white gloves were somehow still clean even after hours on the train.

Miss Donaldina Cameron breathed the damp, salty air and quietly observed her new surroundings. In April of 1895, on the avenues surrounding the San Francisco depot, men with gold-topped walking sticks strode on the boardwalk alongside fashionable, bustle-skirted women. Horse-drawn buggies clattered on cobblestones and streetcars clanged their bells. After a few moments of absorbing the city's atmosphere, Donaldina signaled a horse-drawn cab and sprang up the steps before the driver could give her a hand. She relished the ride, marveling at the modern twelve-story buildings, ornately dressed liverymen outside resplendent hotels, the majestic Ferry Building with its grand clock tower, and beyond it all the glimmer of San Francisco Bay.

As the cab turned north and the street name changed from Grant to Dupont, Donaldina watched California transform into China before her eyes. Bold red and gold Chinese characters appeared on buildings. Wooden tenements, stacked one on top of another, were interlaced with rickety fire escapes, and laundry hung from small balconies. Gone were the pedestrians decked with the top hats and adorned with Victorian dresses; instead, men with long braids under black bowler hats walked in soft cloth shoes or sat in doorways smoking cigars. Boxes of vegetables balanced on uneven wooden sidewalks, and roasted ducks hung by their feet in windows. Donaldina peered into narrow alleyways that criss-crossed the streets. Her nose tingled with whiffs of charcoal, cigar smoke, fried food, and other smells that she did not recognize.

Soon the driver announced, "920 Sacramento Street." He gallantly tipped his cap to Donaldina, then lowered his voice, "Have a care around these parts, ma'am." Then off he drove, leaving her standing on the street gazing up at a formidable brick building. She paused for a moment, looking at her destination, noticing that it was built into the slope of a steep hill and that some of the windows were barred with iron grating. Her feet moved with tempered excitement up several stairs into the shade of the arched entryway, and she put her gloved hand to the knocker. The door opened slowly and a young Chinese woman asked, "Who are you, please?"

"Miss Cameron, the new sewing teacher."

For One Year

The doorkeeper nodded and opened the large oak door to let Donaldina step in; then she closed and bolted it again.

A figure leaped up from a teak chair in the entryway with a cry of "Dolly!" Donaldina was swept up in the embrace of her old friend Eleanor Olney. Eleanor was another of Mrs. Browne's recruits; she did not live at the home but came to teach.

"Dolly! Oh, you look marvelous! And I guess we have had a bit of jolly happenstance! Since Miss Culbertson is all locked up in a meeting, she asked me to welcome you and show you around the house." Eleanor took Donaldina's arm and led her on a tour of the home. They traversed through corridor after corridor, where Donaldina had her first look at many small bedrooms, several busy classrooms, and the large dining hall. When they reached the kitchen, Donaldina saw several young women chopping vegetables and scrubbing large pots. They stopped their work and looked at her. Some had warm, welcoming eyes; others seemed to flinch with fear or flash a challenge of suspicious hostility. Donaldina felt slightly queasy, as if she was slipping into a deep pool of dark eyes. She felt uncomfortably out of place.

After they left the kitchen, Donaldina expressed her puzzled surprise at the dark, sad, suspicion that emanated from some of the women. "Eleanor, what made those women look so sullenly at me?"

Eleanor started to explain how difficult it was to win the trust of those who had been repeatedly deceived and abused. "It takes a world of patience," she sighed. "Well, here is your room, my dear! I wish I could stay with you and talk for hours, but I need to go teach now."

So Donaldina was left alone. Her new bedroom was small but immaculately clean, and her luggage had been delivered. She gravitated towards the window and gazed out, as mesmerized as two-year-old Dolly had been when she pressed her face to a hotel window to watch Chinese men walk through the rain to a cigar factory. A hodgepodge of roofs spread out below her, and men sauntered by or loitered in clusters. There were no women or children in sight.

After a few minutes, Donaldina pulled herself from the window to start unpacking the clothes her sister had so lovingly pressed just one day ago. Just one day, and yet a world away. Her unpacking was interrupted by a knock on the door. A red-haired, freckled young lady smiled shyly and laid a bouquet of white roses in Donaldina's arms.

"Hello! I'm Anna Culbertson, Miss Culbertson's niece. Welcome to San Francisco!" Donaldina beamed radiantly at Anna. She was always ready to respond to an offer of friendship. And she loved roses. She buried her face in the bouquet and breathed the familiar, reassuring fragrance.

Later that afternoon, Miss Culbertson sent for her new assistant. Walking into the superintendent's office, Donaldina extended her hand to the thin, middle-aged woman who stood up from a desk to greet her. Miss Culbertson apologized for not being available earlier, explaining that she was in the middle of a particularly stressful time. She motioned Donaldina to a chair, and when they were both seated, the superintendent plunged directly into conversation.

"I feel I must apprise you of the risks you will take if you cast your lot with us."

Donaldina's brow furrowed in perplexity. "What do you mean?" she asked.

Miss Culbertson spoke clearly, crisply. "This morning, an assortment of sticks was discovered on our front porch and in the grating of some of the windows. Police informed us that it was dynamite, enough to blow up a city block. We haven't uncovered the perpetrator and probably never will, but the last slave girl we rescued was very valuable, and her owners lost a large sum of money through our interference. We have enemies in Chinatown."

As Donaldina absorbed this information, Miss Culbertson carefully drew from a drawer a thin sheet of paper and handed it across the desk, explaining, "This is the translation of a letter recently delivered to us." Donaldina took it and read:

For One Year

Your religion is vain. It costs too much money. By what authority do you rescue girls? If there is any more of this work there will be a contest and blood may flow. Then we will see who is the strongest. We send you this warning. To all Christian teachers.

A grim expression settled on Donaldina's face. Her countenance hardened into what friends would later call her granite look as she raised her head and met the gaze of Miss Culbertson.

"This work entails more than you might have thought," the superintendent continued. "These girls have been taken out of terrible lives of abuse and degradation. They have been treated as chattel. Some are responsive to our care and to the education and opportunities we provide, but others seem unable to break from their wretched past. Some are addicted to opium when they arrive; it is a daunting battle to release them from its grip. They are not quickly healed. I can tell you with great certainty that this is not an easy job, nor is it often very glamorous." She paused. "Would you still like to continue?"

Donaldina's response was succinct. "Are you going to continue?" she asked.

"Of course," replied Miss Culbertson.

"Then I will, too."

A faint smile crossed Miss Culbertson's weary face. "Then why don't I suggest that we go to the staff dining room. I will tell you more over dinner."

Shortly after they sat at the table, a Chinese teenager delivered plates of food, slipping a shy, friendly glance to the new teacher. Just as they started to eat, the doorkeeper who had let Donaldina into the house entered quickly and handed Miss Culbertson a folded note. The superintendent opened and read it, then immediately rose from her chair. Briskly, she told Donaldina, "A girl is in trouble. I must go, please excuse me." To the doorkeeper she said, "Tell Ah Cheng to get her wrap and meet me at the door at once." Donaldina started to rise, too, then sat, not certain what was expected of her. She watched the bustle, wishing she had been asked to go with them. She ate a few bites of dinner, then hovered near the entry hall, waiting for Miss Culbertson to return.

It was perhaps twenty minutes before footsteps echoed on the stairs outside, and the sturdy door was opened to Miss Culbertson and her interpreter, who between them supported a trembling teenager. Donaldina wondered at the sight, bewildered by the girl's colorful, shimmering satin and glamorously painted eyes. Miss Culbertson asked Ah Cheng to take the girl to the kitchen for food, and Donaldina watched wordlessly as the two young women retreated slowly down the hall. Miss Culbertson hung her cloak on a hook by the door and looked at her new resident with an expression grim and weary and yet kind. "It's best for her own countrywomen to help her now," she said. "Come into my office. I'll send for some hot chocolate and we'll talk."

Before they even sat down, Donaldina blurted out, "What kind of slave was that girl?"

Miss Culbertson replied briefly, "A prostitute."

Donaldina was shocked. She had never heard that scandalous word spoken aloud by respectable persons such as Miss Culbertson. "Why..." she began tentatively, unsure of how to voice her questions.

"Were you not told about our work?"

"Yes, I knew there were slaves, but I thought they were orphan girls and household slaves."

Miss Culbertson took a deep breath as she looked out of her window into the darkening dusk of Sacramento Street. "Orphans, yes, and worse." She then told her new assistant the tale that you, dear reader, are already familiar with, the story of the gold miners who came from China, and railroad workers, and how they now lived in San Francisco without wives or families; the story of how Americans exploited Chinese as cheap labor but resisted accepting them as fellow Americans; the story of how the Chinese grew addicted to opium, gambling, and prostitution; the story of how the tong gangs got rich by selling girls; the story of how these girls, used by their own countrymen as well as Americans, suffered unbearably.

While Miss Culbertson spoke, one of the home's residents—Donaldina had seen so many that day in passing, but could not yet recognize most of them—arrived with a tray that held two steaming cups of hot chocolate. Donaldina wrapped her fingers around her cup and listened to the rest of Miss Culbertson's disturbing tale. When she finished, the superintendent reached across her desk and grasped a thick, black ledger. She explained that this was the record of the home's residents, with short accounts of how each of the girls arrived, what circumstances they came from, when and why they left. She handed the book to Donaldina, who set down her cup to hold it in both hands. She opened the cover, and with mingled fascination and horror paged through. She read of an opium addict who could not eat or sleep without the drug and was likely to return to the brothel. She read of a girl who had arrived at the home badly beaten, with wounds that included cuts from a hatchet. She read of another brought to the home for a few days until her deportation back to China, and of another staying for safekeeping before her wedding. Quietness settled over the room while she read.

It had been dark outside for some time now; Donaldina read by yellow gas lamp and candle. She remembered that Miss Culbertson's day had begun with dynamite and ended with an outing into the streets to find a prostitute and carry her to the house. She handed the ledger back to Miss Culbertson, thanked her, expressed her desire to be helpful, and said good night.

As Donaldina slipped into bed, a kaleidoscope of new images swirled in her mind. It seemed to be eons and ages ago that she had jauntily tied on her veil and said farewell to her dear sisters and brother. They had been reluctant to let their beloved Dolly go on this venture, but finally relented, with the understanding that she would be back in a year. One year would surely pass quickly. Donaldina remembered her last night at home on the safe, snug ranch with her family, frog song and rustling trees serenading her outside the window. Tonight, if she looked out, she would see flickering street lamps and hear wafting up an occasional jangling cable car and perhaps snatches of men talking in Cantonese. Under the roof with her were young women her own age who had been deliberately hurt. And there had been dynamite on the stairs she had so perkily ascended that morning.

Donaldina's eldest sister, motherly Annie, had warned her to be careful of the dangers of San Francisco. If only she knew.

Donaldina Cameron at age twenty-five, the year she began work at 920.

Chapter Six
Passing the Baton

老母

*Strength of my heart, I need not fail,
Not mine to fear but to obey,
With such a Leader, who could quail?
Thou art as Thou wert yesterday.
Strength of my heart, I rest in Thee,
Fulfill Thy purposes through me.*
Amy Carmichael

Donaldina pinned on her brooch, patted down a stray hair, emerged from the shelter of her room, and strode down the stairs, resolved to do well on the first day of her new job. She joined Miss Culbertson and Anna for breakfast in the small dining room, where they discussed the household's daily routine. Prayer and Bible classes gave the girls and women opportunity to know the Christian God. Household chores trained them in skills that would help them live on their own. Education equipped them to stand as confident, literate women, whether they stayed in the United States or returned to China. Vocational training, such as the sewing classes that Donaldina would teach, prepared them to provide for themselves.

Fierce Compassion

After breakfast, Donaldina followed Miss Culbertson and Anna to the dining hall. Girls, teenagers, and young women sat at round tables. They were neatly dressed with black hair combed meticulously back. Some chattered amongst themselves while others leaned quietly over their bowls, focused on breakfast. Miss Culbertson walked to the front of the room while Donaldina stayed back, looking in vain for the prostitute who had walked through the door so frightened the night before. The girls laid down their chopsticks and turned toward their leader, and the room was quiet as Miss Culbertson opened a worn copy of the *Book of Common Prayer* and read passages from Psalms and Isaiah. Heads bowed and Miss Culbertson prayed, concluding with a petition that "we may in heart be inspired by thy wisdom, and in work be upheld by thy strength, and in end be accepted of thee as thy faithful servants; through Jesus Christ our Saviour. Amen."

Miss Culbertson dismissed everyone to their morning chores while Donaldina slipped downstairs to become acquainted with the sewing room where she would teach. An hour later, she took a deep breath and stepped into another room to observe Miss Culbertson's class.

Girls filled the neat rows of desks. The youngest looked to be six or seven years old, and the oldest in her middle teens. All eyes focused on the new teacher, who studied the faces turned toward her. As the day before in the kitchen, a few looked inviting and curious while others seemed sullen or devoid of expression.

Miss Culbertson entered the room and commanded the attention of the students. "Girls, this is Miss Cameron. She will be your sewing instructor, and I expect you to show her all the attention and respect that you show me." Donaldina opened her mouth to speak, but Miss Culbertson's hand subtly motioned her to stop.

The superintendent looked carefully and deliberately over the class. "I have a serious matter to discuss with you." Her face hardened with severity. "Someone has taken the apples that we were saving as a special treat to share." She paused and her steely gaze scanned the

Passing the Baton

room. "Who stole the apples?" Donaldina flinched at the superintendent's tone.

Miss Culbertson repeated the question. After a fearful silence, a round and rosy-cheeked girl, about twelve years old, slowly stood. The pools gathering in her eyes began to overflow. "I did it," she whispered.

"Tien!" exclaimed Miss Culbertson.

The girl's lips trembled as she confessed. Later, she admitted that some others had convinced her to take the apples, telling her they would share the blame if she were caught. But now no one owned up to the deed, and Tien stood alone. Later that day, Donaldina, impressed by Tien's honesty and sympathetic to her plight, went to the ledger book to see if she could find the girl's story. She paged through until she reached an entry, dated a year earlier, and read the story of Tien Wu, who had been scooped up into the arms of a police officer on a rainy January afternoon. *...Another method of torture was to dip lighted candlewicking in oil and burn her arms with it. Teen Fook is a pretty child of about ten years old, rosy cheeked and fair complexion...*

Donaldina determined that moment to make friends with Tien Wu, starting with her first sewing class that afternoon. But Tien Wu avoided the new teacher, refusing to make eye contact and shaking off any affectionate touch. Every friendly gesture that Miss Cameron made was rebuffed, and strong-willed Tien Wu intentionally sewed badly for her teacher that afternoon.

On a windy April evening a few days after Donaldina's arrival, the doorkeeper again came to Miss Culbertson with a piece of paper. The superintendent read it and slipped it in her dress. "Miss Cameron," she said, "I need to go help a girl in distress. Care to join me?"

A rush of excitement pulsed through Donaldina's blood. She quickly wrapped herself in a cloak and left the shelter of the home with Miss Culbertson and Ah Cheng. They hurried down Sacramento Street. Donaldina noticed with apprehensive thrill the sledgehammers and axes wielded by the police officers who met them at the bottom of the hill.

They hastened along the sidewalk, dodging clusters of men, and Donaldina vaguely wondered what thoughts lurked behind the sidelong glances cast in their direction. They turned into narrow Bartlett Alley, scouring doorposts for addresses–Donaldina tripped on a pile of vegetable scraps–and then they stopped at a door of rotting wood and peeling paint. Vigorous pounding yielded no reply. Anyone who might have been out in the alley had vanished into the shadows. The oddly sinister quiet was pierced by the shrill whistle of one of the policemen, and after a short wait, three more officers came running.

Donaldina stepped back, trying to keep out of the way. The police pried off the metal grating from a lower window and broke the glass. They climbed through the window, the women maneuvering their dresses over shattered glass. As her eyes adjusted to the dim light, Donaldina saw a small and sparsely furnished room, dank and dark, smelling of trash. Then she spotted a person cowering on the floor in the corner, her face eerily lit by a single candle. Donaldina watched as in a single, decisive movement Miss Culbertson rushed to the woman, knelt down, grasped her hands and said, "We are from the mission." The trembling girl shrank back for a moment, and then said, "Yes, I come. I come."

Angry shouting resounded in the hall, and the bulk of a man loomed in the doorway. Comprehension of his Cantonese was not required to understand that he was enraged. He slammed the door and they found themselves face-to-face with him, access to the window blocked. He glowered down upon the group, and most ferociously at the girl, who cringed against Miss Culbertson, convulsing with hysteric sobs as the man fixed his eyes on her and lashed her with curses. The police officers moved towards the man and demanded with words and hand motions that he unbolt the door. He sullenly complied, but the clamor of his curses and threats chased them as they hustled out of the building and into the alleyway. Ah Cheng and Miss Culbertson supported the woman, with Donaldina following, and the five policemen formed a protective circle around them. They scurried back through the alley, into the busy thoroughfare and up the hill.

Dark and fog had settled on the city by the time they arrived, panting, at the home. The cold air reddened Donaldina's cheeks, but the excitement and the quick stride up the steep hill had warmed her. Donaldina Mackenzie Cameron, for the first time in her life, had stepped into one of the dark, frightful corners of Chinatown and broken into a locked building. She had faced a yelling slave owner and taken part in rescuing a slave—a trembling, trampled woman about her own age who desperately needed help. And though Donaldina felt small and weak in the face of this terror, a desire was already growing in her to do it again.

Gradually the new sewing teacher found her place in the daily pattern of the home. She participated with other staff in the rhythm of prayer, meals, chores, and classes. She soon knew the individual faces, names, and personalities of girls who had all looked alike to her at first, and bit-by-bit she won their affection and trust. Some still glared at her or looked down to avoid her friendly gaze, but others started to smile shyly, and the littlest girls soon ardently ran to her and climbed into her lap whenever she was in sight.

Amidst routines of classes and work, Donaldina learned more about the forces that surrounded this refuge. She asked questions, and she opened her eyes and ears. She learned more about American racism that beleaguered her new neighbors and tong brutality that terrorized them. She started to recognize Cantonese swear words from the angry ravings and coarse behavior of some of her new housemates. She shuddered at their suffering. A fifteen-year-old had open wounds from beatings and burns inflicted at the brothel. A young woman her own age could not sleep, feverish and ulcerated from syphilis. Donaldina sat next to the beds of women who were vomiting from opium withdrawal. And these were only the visible scars. Other hurts were buried deep in memories of shame and abuse, not easy to draw out and heal.

Donaldina was horrified, but her repugnance did not push her away. Instead, her resolved compassion was strengthened. And though she was shocked by the vileness, she was also inspired by the astounding transformations she witnessed. "Some of the newly rescued girls come in as forlorn, dejected looking creatures, either too frightened, or else too sullen even to smile," she reflected "But how truly wonderful it is to see how rapidly they respond to kind words and gentle treatment."

Spring turned to summer and summer to autumn, and the house on the hill depended more and more on its new assistant. Miss Cameron charmed the small children, who were instinctively drawn to her. She taught well, was skillful in administration, and was soon known to be boldly courageous on rescue missions. She learned how to nurse measles and whooping cough and syphilis. She became an astute student of the complexities of corrupt San Francisco politics and the clever tricks of the tongs. She communicated charmingly and clearly to the home's American and Chinese visitors. She learned quickly, loved enthusiastically, and lifted many burdens off the exhausted shoulders of Miss Culbertson. Her contagious cheerfulness infused the home with a new joy.

Donaldina also built trust with the Board of Directors who cared so deeply about the mission of 920. At Donaldina's first annual board meeting, the long-time leaders of the mission observed her carefully. When one of the younger girls bounded off the platform after a Scripture recitation, running over to climb confidently onto Miss Cameron's lap, it was enough to endear Donaldina to the Board. Miss Culbertson's emphatic endorsement of Donaldina's invaluable assistance further convinced them.

With the return of spring, Donaldina's promised year at the home was nearly over. Her family in the south happily anticipated her return. Shortly before the year elapsed, she was summoned to Miss Culbertson's office.

"Donaldina," began Miss Culbertson, "the Board has asked me to request that you continue to work with us. I, too, request that you stay. You know as well as I do that we cannot afford to pay you what you are worth to us—only twenty-five dollars a month, and you'll have to pay for your room and board. It is a meager offering, but do try to remember how important this work is, and how well suited you are for it. We all rely so heavily upon you and your youthful vivacity."

Donaldina did not meet Miss Culbertson's gaze; her thoughts were elsewhere. Never had this beloved youngest Cameron been away from her family for so long. During the nights, when she lay awake listening to the sounds of the city, she remembered the fresh air and rolling hills of her brother's ranch home. Did she really want to spend the rest of her youth toiling as an underpaid assistant in this crowded, tumultuous place? Chances for meeting a husband here were quite slim, were they not? She had talents and resources, did she not? Surely she could do many other things besides help at a Chinese orphanage and safe house. Or was this God's call on her life? If it was, then she must follow the path he was calling her to. If she stayed, it would certainly not be for any monetary incentive: twenty-five dollars was close to the minuscule wage that the Chinese railroad workers had been paid several decades ago. But her heart balked at the thought of leaving the girls she had come to love. And if she left, who would take her place?

Miss Culbertson had stopped talking, and Donaldina's conflicting thoughts merged into a simple reply, "Thank you, Miss Culbertson. I will seriously consider this and inform you of my decision as soon as possible."

"Thank you, Donaldina."

Short days later, while Donaldina was still wondering what she should do, she was surprised by a visitor. Cheerful Charles Bailey, husband of her sister Jesse, had come to escort her home. She was so glad to see him, and into his sympathetic ear she poured out her confused dilemma about whether she should return home or continue working in San Francisco. That evening, Charlie joined the mission house staff for a jovial dinner, and Donaldina went to bed with a lightened heart. She told Charlie she would tell him her decision the next day.

When Donaldina woke that next day, she knew what she was going to do. She would ask for a vacation at home with her family. Then she would return to her work at 920. When permission for the two-week vacation was granted, Donaldina was ecstatic. She practically ran down the street to shop: a flat sailor hat for herself and a cheerful muslin dress for each sister.

On the train ride south, Donaldina and Charlie were stopped by an unusual April snowstorm. They stepped outside and Charlie showed her how to make snowballs. At home, Donaldina enjoyed two glorious weeks of horseback riding, picnics, and parties with friends. She returned to San Francisco invigorated and ready to work.

Throughout the next year, Donaldina toiled alongside Miss Culbertson. She loved the girls and women living in the home, in all their stages of upheaval and healing, and she continued to learn more about the workings of San Francisco's politics and Chinatown's organized crime.

The activity at 920 Sacramento Street increasingly threatened the power of those in the business of buying and selling girls. Donaldina was amazed by the tricks that the slave owners used to keep their grip on their property. To prevent slaves from being discovered, they stashed them in secret spaces under floors or in compartments built into false ceilings. To keep their slaves from running away, they warned them of horrors that would befall them in the house on the hill–white missionaries who drank the blood and ate the organs of Chinese girls. If, despite these strategies, a slave made it to the home, the owner's tong would try to recover her. If threats or attempts at kidnapping did not work, they went to the police, claiming that the runaway had committed a crime. As soon as their woman was in jail, they took her out on bail; after that, she was likely whisked away through an elaborate network of alliances, never to be seen again.

Tong godfathers cultivated relationships with the police assigned to Chinatown, some of whom were happy to supplement their income with diamonds or handfuls of gold coins and then pass on information when they heard that Miss Culbertson or Miss Cameron was planning a rescue. San Francisco politics were famously corrupt, and some lawyers and city politicians were also bribed by the tongs.

Donaldina Cameron, the naïve country girl, was growing cunning. She identified police officers and lawyers and judges whom she suspected were not corruptible and who wanted to promote genuine justice for the Chinese. Her persuasive eloquence gradually won allies who joined her in pushing back against Chinatown's brutal and illegal slave trade. And she had a weapon more powerful than any of the tongs' hatchets or gold: a deep and compassionate love for the girls in her care. That love made her fierce. She fumed whenever a police officer walked out of the house escorting a girl to jail while the innocent-looking Chinese accuser subtly smirked. She became enraged whenever she received a plea for help and then rushed to the address only to find a recently abandoned room, its occupants having been warned by a bribed police officer who had heard of the rescue plan. Donaldina Cameron would not be bullied and she would not be outwitted. She was determined to protect her girls.

At the end of Donaldina's second year in San Francisco, Margaret Culbertson wrote in the annual board report that "Miss Cameron, our valued assistant, is still at her post and has proven herself a tower of strength by her cheerful and faithful discharge of the many and ofttimes perplexing duties that fall to her hand." Recognizing that the home was secure in the hands of this assistant, Miss Culbertson's friends and colleagues persuaded her to take a sabbatical. But by then, she had worked beyond what her health could sustain. A few days after saying goodbye to her household, while traveling on a train to the east coast, Margaret Culbertson died.

Donaldina grieved. And she worried. She suspected that the Board would ask her to become the next superintendent, and did not feel ready to accept full responsibility for the household of fifty girls. She quailed under the strain, writing that "the beginning of the year was fraught with misgivings." So board member Mrs. Fields agreed to act as temporary director of the home with the understanding that Donaldina would soon take the position.

The tongs knew about Miss Culbertson's death, and they looked for an opportunity to capitalize on a time of potential weakness in the home. They were starting to realize that the new, young missionary would not back down without a fight. Donaldina Cameron's lithe figure was increasingly recognized in the streets and alleys of Chinatown. In fact, Donaldina Cameron had a new nickname, whispered in brothels and gambling rooms across Chinatown: Fahn Quai, Foreign Devil. To destroy the home, they would have to get Fahn Quai out of the way.

One day, Donaldina received a message allegedly from a slave, begging for rescue. She hurried out of the protective doors of 920 and zig-zagged back and forth toward her destination. Dark was descending as she turned into the malodorous alley and entered the apartment. Rushing through the open door, she suddenly halted and felt a sickening thud in her stomach. There was no girl cringing in the corner here. Instead, she saw an effigy, a model of herself, hanging in the dim room. It dangled from a beam, swaying slightly. And thrust in its heart was a dagger.

Fuming, Donaldina retraced her steps back to 920. Her lips formed a firm line and a granite expression settled on her face. This morbid threat would not intimidate her. She assured herself with the bold reasoning that "those who intend to do violence act. They do not give warning." (Astute readers might remember that the tongs did sometimes give warning, posted on Chinatown streets, before their murders—Donaldina might have been unaware of this, or perhaps she was very bravely bluffing.)

Meanwhile, the girls and young women in the home increasingly came to Donaldina with their worries and joys. Young girls begged her for permission for late-night snacks. Older ones tossed in her bed as she nursed them through the night; when they were tormented with nightmares, they looked to her for comfort. She gave her best to crafting 920 Sacramento Street into a place of safety and love. In the upper rooms of tong clubhouses, Donaldina Cameron was called Fahn Quai. But in the home, she would soon be given another nickname, a colloquial Cantonese term of endearment that would follow her the rest of her life: "Lo Mo," translated literally as "Old Mother."

At the end of another full day, Donaldina gathered herself together for a few quiet moments alone in her room, gazing out at the lamp-lit city as she thought with mixed fondness, joy, and worry of the girls under the roof with her. It was nearly the end of 1899, and Donaldina Cameron had accepted the role of Superintendent of the Mission Home for Chinese Girls and Women. Miss Culbertson and Mrs. Fields had run their races as hard as they could, and had passed the baton to her, trusting her to continue.

Donaldina knelt in prayer beside her bed. She smiled as she thought of little Dong Ho, who had recently appeared at the home. This brave girl fled from her abusive owner one Sunday morning and set out alone to find the mission house. She wandered the streets most of the day, terrified of being captured and returned. By late afternoon, she stood in front of a large house, wondering if it was the mission. She nervously walked up the stairs and rang the bell. It was not the mission house, but was only a half block away, and the woman who answered brought the terrified, exhausted girl to 920. Soon after

Dong Ho's arrival, her small friend Suey Leen, who had been pawned to the same owner to pay a debt, also escaped to the home. The two of them loved to sit together in bed and tell sympathetic new friends about their troubles.

Tomorrow would bring more hard work and danger. It was daunting. But Donaldina also had reason to hope for triumph and joy. In one of the early reports she wrote as superintendent, she revealed the source of her confidence, sharing from the book of Isaiah that "the Lord's hand is not shortened that it cannot save, neither is his ear heavy that he cannot hear." As the 1800s drew to a close, the Superintendent of the Mission Home trusted God's protective arm to hold her and her tumultuous household.

920 Sacramento Street

Chapter Seven
Death and Life in a New Century

果決

Speak up for those who cannot speak for themselves,
For the rights of all who are destitute.
Proverbs 31:8

On December 31, 1899, San Franciscans celebrated the bright promise of a new century. Bedazzling gowns and dashing tuxedos sparkled at lavish balls, and city streets clamored with bells, whistles, and tin horns. Spirits were only slightly dampened when the Chief of Police lined each block with ten extra uniformed men whose job it was to prevent indiscriminate public kissing.

Several weeks later, the Chinese would prepare for their own festivities. Chinese New Year is indubitably the most festive time of year, and Chinatown never failed (and indeed still never fails) to greet the holiday with all-out merrymaking. The holiday generates days upon days of colorfully bannered streets, fireworks to light the night, noisy parades with long dragons and lion dances, lavish feasting, and high spirits. But in January of 1900, the days leading up to the New Year were shrouded with a grim pall: "Instead of fireworks, gunfire rang through the streets, and the alleys ran with blood. Gang warfare had struck again." Police moved into Chinatown to clamp down on tong violence. All public holiday celebrations were canceled

And then the rats came to Chinatown. They came in hordes. They died in hordes. The streets reeked of rank rat remains. Representatives from Chinatown's civic associations asked the city of San Francisco to remove the carcasses, but were ignored. When there was an outbreak of dying rats in rural China, people fled. But in San Francisco, there was nowhere to go. The rodents seemed to be a sinister omen of death for this new year–the Year of the Rat.

Lumber salesman Wong Chut King woke up one morning too weak to go to work. He collapsed into a bunk in his cramped room on Dupont Street. Soon his high fever and severe abdominal pain made him delirious then pushed him into a coma. His organs began hemorrhaging and his blood pressure plunged. A corpse in the house was considered bad luck, so one of his fellow-boarders told the landlord, and Wong Chut King was dragged to a coffin shop, where he died. A police surgeon came in to examine the body. The diagnosis: bubonic plague.

Immediately, America's public health officials focused their attention on San Francisco. Infectious disease experts hypothesized that the rats had scuttled off a ship from Hong Kong or Honolulu, which were both fighting outbreaks of plague. The rats, with plague-infested fleas living in their fur, made themselves at home in Chinatown. After the bacteria killed the rats, the fleas found human hosts.

The menace of plague terrified San Francisco's politicians and businessmen. The bustling, modern, up-and-coming city of San Francisco must not be decimated by the plague! Scientists and the public suspected that Chinese were more susceptible to the disease than Caucasians (they are not) and they feared that the Chinese would catch the plague and spread it across San Francisco.

In an attempt to stop this threat, American public health officials descended on Chinatown to collect and cremate bodies. But the Chinese dreaded cremation, so they surreptitiously dragged bodies out of Chinatown to avoid the sacrilegious burning. Police conducted door-to-door searches for corpses. Meanwhile, the disinfectant of choice, sulfur-burning pots, permeated Chinatown with overpoweringly smoky stench, and the odor of rotting rats was supplemented by the pungency of rotting eggs.

Twice during the plague scare, the public health department quarantined Chinatown. Police guarded a blockade; no one was allowed in or out. The blockade line zig-zagged: a few Caucasian-owned stores that cut into those blocks were excused from the quarantine since they were, after all, white. The quarantine wreaked havoc. Thousands who usually traveled in and out of Chinatown each day to their jobs in other parts of the city were stranded. As the quarantine continued, isolated Chinatown residents went hungry. Some panicked. They ran up and down along the line looking for a way out.

The mission home lay just outside the western edge of the quarantine and was therefore cut off from the rest of Chinatown. Yet one dismal, dreary day, a bedraggled little girl broke the blockade and came running through the pouring rain up the steps of 920. Water ran from her thin dress to the floor of the entryway as she told her story to the interpreter, with heaving breaths puncturing her fragmented sentences. Her sister was terribly sick and had been left in the rain to perish alone. Could someone please help?

The sobs of the dripping girl drew Donaldina to the front hall. She instantly began to form a plan of action. A few minutes later, she was several blocks away, quietly slipping through the door of an herbalist who lived on the edge of the quarantine and was, conveniently, deeply grateful to her for rescuing his wife. He found a costume to conceal Donaldina's Scottish features, and they climbed up to the top floor. Out of the skylight into the rain emerged an ancient-looking Chinese woman, hunched under a black umbrella. That very same old lady somehow deftly scurried from rooftop to rooftop, in the rain, to the skylight of another friend who lived inside the quarantine line. She pulled the window open, lowered herself, and went hurrying down the street in her disguise.

Donaldina reached the building the girl had described and saw the sister lying abandoned in the rain, hot with fever and struggling to breathe. Even the intrepid Donaldina realized that transporting the limp body back over the roofs of Chinatown would be a near impossibility, so she returned to 920 by the same route she had come. At home, she went straight for the telephone, called the Board of Health, and demanded that an ambulance be sent immediately. Whether because of the authority in Miss Cameron's voice or the public health department's desire to secure as many plague corpses as possible, an ambulance soon drove through the quarantine line and the girl was fetched back to 920 for treatment. Everyone waited with bated breath, wondering if 920 would witness its first case of bubonic plague. But the doctor did not diagnose plague–the girl had appendicitis. What would have been treatable a few hours earlier was now beyond medical help. Ah Ching was at her sister's side when death arrived.

"Lo Mo," the bereaved Ah Ching whispered to Donaldina through the translator, "I don't want to go back there. Let me stay here with you." Donaldina went to work to obtain legal guardianship of Ah Ching, and the girl spent the rest of her childhood and youth at 920. She flourished and soon became a source of companionship and help right up until the day, years later, when Donaldina proudly, sadly waved goodbye. The poised young woman on the steamer ship was embarking on a journey back to her homeland to work as a kindergarten teacher.

Donaldina and her staff and household were still recovering from the chaos and anxiety of the tong outburst and plague scare when Kum Qui arrived. Two years earlier, a slave traders had brought seventy Chinese teens and young women into the country, using the World Fair in Omaha as a ruse. These lovely "cultural ambassadors" smiled at visitors to the fair's model Chinese village. Afterwards, instead of returning to China, they disappeared into the brothels of the West Coast, where they were sold as prostitutes. Kum Qui was one of these women. She had been found soon after trying to kill herself, and was brought to 920. Fearful and frantic at first, she started to feel more at ease in her new home each day.

One never knew what a day would bring at 920 Sacramento Street. A week after Kum Qui's arrival, a loud knock resounded. Donaldina opened the door to a burly constable and an inscrutable Chinese man; she recognized neither of them. The constable thrust out a photo. "Ma'am, we have a warrant to arrest this girl for theft of jewelry."

Donaldina looked at the photo and inwardly breathed a sigh of relief, "I'm sorry, sir, but you've made a mistake. I know every girl who lives here, and that girl most definitely does not."

"Well, you won't mind if we have a look," was the constable's terse reply. And so lessons stopped and word went out that everyone was to gather in the chapel for inspection. The household was ready for these visits. Anyone being pursued was hustled off and concealed in the cracks of the folding doors, or behind rice bags, or in holes in the basement. But this time, no one recognized the new, clever trick–the photo was a hoax, and the woman in the picture was not the woman whose name was on the warrant. Kum Qui lined up with her new friends before she saw her former owner. Donaldina watched Kum Qui's face blanch and realized that they had been duped.

Donaldina beseeched the officer not to take Kum Qui, to no avail. The younger girls began to cry. Kum Qui clung to Lo Mo before the officer jerked her away. Donaldina hesitated very briefly. Then she impulsively bolted out the door after Kum Qui and the two men. The interpreter frantically gave chase, holding out Lo Mo's hat and coat.

Donaldina was determined to stay with Kum Qui. Undoubtedly, the police officer and slave owner were exasperated at this interfering missionary, but they let her come, having no other choice other than making a public scene. They were planning a fifty-mile trip south to San Jose for the trial, but stopped in Palo Alto for the night. Kum Qui was taken to the local jail cell, a damp shed furnished with two boxes and some filthy blankets. Donaldina stepped in after her. The door bolted behind them. Donaldina reached over and grasped Kum Qui's hand. Though they had little language in common, Kum Qui knew in the depths of her heart that this woman loved her and would not let her return to her tormented slavery.

In the darkest hour of night, Donaldina woke with a start to the sound of shuffling outside. The door was forced open, and shadowy shapes appeared. Donaldina was on her feet to shield Kum Qui, but even the feisty Scotswoman could not stop three men from overpowering her and dragging their prize out the door. Kum Qui's terrified scream provoked livid anger in Lo Mo. She chased them to their buggy and hurled herself in, but once more the strength of three men proved to be too much. They pushed her out and drove away triumphantly, and she was left fuming in the dust.

Donaldina picked herself up and ran back toward Palo Alto for help. Meanwhile, Kum Qui's abductors met with a judge who had agreed to preside over the case by the side of the road at 2:30 in the morning. This unscrupulous judge declared Kum Qui guilty of theft. Her abductors paid her five-dollar bail and then rushed off with her, north to San Francisco. There, Kum Qui was forced, under threat of death, to marry a stranger. This marriage would make it easier to transport her across the country. She was then taken to the train depot to be sent far from San Francisco and the white missionary's prying ways. But, of course, Donaldina had not yet given up. A friend helped her trace the abductors. To the shock of Kum Qui's owners, Donaldina Cameron met them personally at the train station, policemen at her side. They arrested the whole group: Kum Qui, her "husband," and the kidnappers.

Finally, a judge, interpreter, clerks, witnesses, and defendants assembled in court for a more legitimate trial. Kum Qui must have been very beautiful indeed, for her owners tenaciously tried to recover her again. At one point in the trial, a constable requested that Kum Qui be removed from the courtroom. Perhaps it was his position of authority, perhaps it was because the court did not think that the testimony of a mere Chinese girl was necessary, perhaps it was out of thoughtlessness, but regardless of the reason, Kum Qui was handed over. The moment she was out of sight, the policeman took the exhausted, tremulous woman to a waiting car. She was abducted again. This time, an observant government interpreter bravely gave chase and rescued her. The constable was added to the growing group of defendants now awaiting trial.

The scandalous story leaked. A white woman thrown in jail with her Chinese foster daughter and then cast out onto the road. A suspicious middle-of-the-night roadside trial, followed by a suspicious marriage. A policeman stealing one of the defendants from right under the judge's nose. Professors and students from Stanford University, as well as citizens from Palo Alto, were indignant at the corruption they detected in California's justice system. An agitated crowd congregated in front of the jail shed, threatening to tear it down. A grassroots meeting was arranged to investigate what had happened and discuss the issues it raised of freedom, justice, and Constitutional rights. Donaldina found herself swept up in the public's interest and was asked to give an impromptu speech in front of the hundreds who gathered. She related the entirety of the scandalous story and pleaded on behalf of Kum Qui, who after all of that horrifying ordeal was still held as a prisoner awaiting her third trial on a trumped up charge of theft. The *San Francisco Chronicle* described the speech:

> "Seldom anywhere has a great audience made so wonderful a demonstration of enthusiasm as when Miss Cameron came forward in response to the introduction and told her simple, straightforward story of the experience she had had in attempting to protect her ward…Although low, Miss Cameron's voice was heard in all portions of the room. The speaker proved by her beauty and modest manner that she was a refined and cultured woman, and it seemed amazing how men could subject such a woman to such vile indignities as she related as having been perpetrated at Palo Alto…We admire the fearless, heroic, and womanly action of Miss Cameron in her efforts to prevent the abduction of her ward."

Donaldina Cameron was front-page news. Kum Qui's harrowing adventure swayed public favor toward the work of the mission home. Although Donaldina was glad for more public awareness of the slave trade, she was also concerned that the Chinese would continue to be stereotyped in American eyes, caricatured as crafty thugs or victimized girls. She longed for others to see the personality, talent, and culture she enjoyed in her Chinese family. To this end, she used her eloquent charm, telling stories about her daughters to anyone in her path. She befriended the newsboy, who delighted in watching her dash up and down the hill and noted admiringly that when she was intent on helping someone, she could have "more gall than a burglar." She dined with the highly educated, gentlemanly Chinese consul. Donaldina also took her foster daughters on outings to act as ambassadors to the greater world. Two or three or four at a time, they happily clambered onto cable cars and ferries, attracting curious stares as they travelled all around San Francisco Bay to receptions and meetings. They made friends wherever they went.

Donaldina also greeted the increasingly growing stream of visitors who came from all across the country as the home became more well-known. The housekeeper recorded that 920 hosted an average of twenty to thirty visitors a day during the tourist season. This could create plenty of hassle in the home's routine, but it built good relationships and chipped away at racism.

One visitor threw 920 Sacramento Street into excited uproar. President Theodore Roosevelt was coming! Anticipation animated the classrooms and halls and kitchen and bedrooms as every inch was scoured and scrubbed. No one knew exactly what time the president planned to arrive, and when day turned into night with no news of the esteemed guest, they reluctantly trundled off to bed. Shortly after midnight, a phone call announced that the president's party was finally on its way. Everyone woke up. The kitchen filled with clatter. Girls quickly dressed and combed each other's hair. When President Roosevelt walked through the door, all was ready. The girls, happy and poised, served him refreshments, conversed intelligently, and performed songs and Bible recitations. As the president and his entourage gathered by the door to leave, someone whispered appreciatively to the housekeeper that the girls were "the most charming little people" they had ever met.

President Roosevelt was trying to figure out what to do about Chinese-American issues. He wanted to improve conditions for the Chinese in the United States, but he also wanted to continue restricting their immigration, and had expressed his opinion that the Chinese were an inferior race. We hope that the bright girls and young women at 920 Sacramento Street gave him something to consider that night.

Donaldina Cameron had been working and living at 920 for six years. For more than two thousand days and nights she had shared life with her girls–danger, sorrow and joy, meals and classes and chores. They had celebrated births and weddings together and grieved at funerals. There had been time for relationships to grow deep. Donaldina gave her devotion steadfastly to each girl and woman, and most of them ardently returned her love.

But Tien Wu, the apple thief whom Donaldina had met on her first day, still rejected Lo Mo's friendship. Her rebellion manifested itself in a multitude of ways. Early one morning, in a fit of fury at having been scolded, Tien opened all the windows in her room so the chilly fog could roll in. She discarded most of her clothes and leaned outside. Tien's confused roommate woke up and blearily mumbled, "Tien! What are you doing?"

"Go to another room if you're cold," Tien declared tragically, "I'm going to catch pneumonia and die. Then I will come back as a spirit and torment Miss Cameron. That will teach her to be sorry." But glowering Tien never contracted pneumonia; on the contrary, she seemed to be doomed with good health.

Though Tien, now a teenager, resented Lo Mo, she adored Donaldina's interpreter and assistant, Yuen Qui, a beautiful young lady with a smooth, round face, big black eyes, and a sweet disposition. Yuen Qui was a blessing to everyone in the home. One day, Donaldina discovered her interpreter coughing in the corner. Yuen Qui weakly protested as Donaldina led her to bed. This was no common cold, and soon tuberculosis was confirmed. Yuen Qui lost her appetite, and for weeks tossed restlessly in a feverish sweat. Donaldina wrote of a deep, darkening shadow that fell over the home during her illness.

Death and Life in a New Century

Tien Wu was at the bedside when Yuen Qui died. Terrified, she ran to fetch Lo Mo. Donaldina flew into the room fervently hoping that Tien Wu was mistaken. But when she saw the face that had once been so full of life and light now covered with deathly pallor, she knew that there was no mistake. Donaldina threw herself onto the bed, sobs shaking her entire body. Tien Wu watched closely. The teenager slowly walked over and grasped the hand of her foster mother.

"Don't cry, Lo Mo. I help you."

Thus ended any animosity between Tien Wu and Lo Mo. Tien worked faithfully at the home, helping Donaldina until an opportunity for higher education brought her East. After graduating, she returned to keep her promise to help Lo Mo. Tien dedicated the rest of her life to serving as Donaldina's devoted assistant, and was there with her leader and friend until Donaldina's dying breath many decades later.

Tien Wu (at about age 16) and Yuen Qui in 1900 – the year that Yuen Qui died.

Grieving the loss of Yuen Qui, Donaldina reflected that "her memory will be a constant benediction." The relationship forged between Tien Wu and Donaldina Cameron on her deathbed was surely a part of this benediction.

On rare days of leisure, Donaldina took her daughters out of Chinatown's smog to play in the fresh air of the countryside. Occasionally they went to the coast, where they tied up their skirts and frolicked in the lapping waves of the Pacific. The sand squelched between their toes and they strained their eyes, searching the horizon and wondering about what lay beyond. Many remembered families and friends who lived on the other side of that ocean, threatened by bandits and starvation. Most harbored other dark and frightening memories. Now, woven together into this new family, they danced together on the shore of the sea. To passing strangers, it would appear odd: a dozen Chinese girls with a striking white woman in the middle of them, dancing without shoes and without shame. Dancing for joy and dancing with hope and dancing because love was in their hearts.

Chapter Eight
Of Love and Travel and the Like

盼望

*Accustom yourself to look first to the dreadful consequences of failure;
then fix your eye on the glorious prize which is before you;
and when your strength begins to fail, and your spirits are well nigh
exhausted, let the animating view rekindle your resolution,
and call forth in renewed vigour the fainting energies of your soul.*
William Wilberforce

The house on the hill fluttered with jovial commotion. Daily drudgery was cast aside as armloads of flowers were meticulously arranged in the meeting hall. Tantalizing aromas of frying duck mingled with those of a freshly baked wedding cake, a fragrant representation of the blending of cultural traditions at 920. Upstairs, a bride made herself ready. It was a wedding day.

Donaldina took her role as matchmaker seriously, ever-vigilant in her quest to protect her daughters from illegitimate suitors. Hopeful men had to prove their sincerity and their ability to care for a wife, and they had to convince Lo Mo that they were not henchmen hired to recover an escaped slave. Any admirer who came to declare his intentions had to first pass Lo Mo's interrogation. He was ushered into the meeting room and seated at the formidable table, and the process began. He must provide letters of reference vouching for his good character. He must show that he could support a family. If the young lady of his intentions was a follower of Christ, then he too must be sincere in his devotion to God. Unless the suitor passed Lo Mo's scrutiny, he would be prevented from wooing the woman of his choice. Upon her approval, the couple would enter into a courtship. If all went well, the household relished the delightful anticipation of a wedding.

At times, Lo Mo's matchmaking work was unusually strenuous. Several months before this wedding day, a frightened young tong man named Sin Kee had knocked on the door of 920 desperate for help. He knew a slave girl. She confided her miseries and fears to him. He fell in love with her and promised to care for her if she ran away. She ran. Her owner traced her.

And then, Sin Kee discovered that the owner of his beloved was from a rival tong. This was more than enough provocation to trigger a new wave of violence between the two tongs. To avoid starting a string of murders (beginning with his own), he agreed to an arrangement that was acceptable to the tong code of honor. The owner would hold the slave girl hostage at his headquarters until Sin Kee handed over one thousand dollars to purchase her. Sin Kee tried frantically to collect the huge sum, but it was impossible. Then he thought of Miss Cameron. It was a risky move, for according to the unwritten rules that governed Chinatown, a Chinese man never helped a Chinese slave woman escape. Men had been tortured and killed for helping girls to the home. But Sin Kee saw no other option, and so he furtively went to 920 to beg for Miss Cameron's help.

He found the white woman remarkably sympathetic. The instant he finished his story, the resolute Miss Cameron began to act. She determined the exact whereabouts of the hostage, then grabbed Kum Ching, the interpreter, from window-washing, and out they went on their little adventure. On the way down the hill, Donaldina

Of Love and Travel and the Like

spotted an Irish police officer. He was, perhaps, more corpulent and aged than she would have preferred, but a policeman was a policeman. "Come with us!" Donaldina hollered across the street. They soon arrived at the notorious Ross Alley. Even in broad daylight, ominous shadows seemed to close in on them. Donaldina pointed out the tong headquarters to Kum Ching. As they nonchalantly ambled past, the sleepy doorkeeper failed to see Kum Ching break apart from the group and dash back to the building. He jolted awake and reached up to slam the heavy door, but he was too late. Kum Ching held the door open while Donaldina scrambled in, the policeman puffing up behind them.

A scream pierced the air. Donaldina darted towards the sound. A door slammed. Our friend the policeman figured it would be best if he went searching for more help, so Donaldina and Kum Ching waited for twenty excruciating minutes, standing in the hallway and shuddering at the indistinguishable, muffled sounds coming from the other side of the door.

When three officers arrived and broke in, the room was a picture of peace, with thirteen Chinese men smoking placidly around a table. When asked where the slave woman was, they replied with imperturbable calmness that there were no slave girls there. The women and police searched thoroughly while the men continued to sit, apparently oblivious to their visitors. There was no one being held hostage here. The police, convinced that this time Miss Cameron must be mistaken, were ready to quit. Donaldina, however, disregarding the disapproving glares of the men around the table, opened a window and clambered onto the ledge of the fire escape. A man painting a scaffold across the alley called out, "They took her through the skylight, across the roof next door." Donaldina nodded her thanks, slipped back into the room and then quietly beckoned one of the officers to follow her.

The neighbor opened his door and recognized Fahn Quai. He immediately started protesting that he had a fine Christian home with no slave girls, but had to give way to the police that followed this crazy lady. A ladder was propped up next to the open skylight, a promising sign, but searching remained fruitless until Donaldina noticed a dresser that was slightly out of line with the wall. A face peeked out from behind this piece of furniture and a timid voice queried, "Mission Home?" The terrified but relieved girl allowed Donaldina to escort her out as thirteen infuriated men gathered themselves to chase this exasperating woman and regain their property.

When the group emerged into the daylight, they discovered a group of tourists in the alley below. The group's guide looked at the oddly matched group, made a guess about what was happening, and explained it to the others, who energetically cheered for the slave victim and her rescuers. The defeated owners "slunk quickly out of sight, struck with terror themselves at the sound of this unexpected demonstration." Another of Lo Mo's matchmaking duties was successfully accomplished.

Sin Kee and his beloved would have a happy future, but today's celebration was not for them. This wedding's bride was a radiant young lady who had been rescued years earlier when she was still a child slave. She was marrying a wealthy businessman from southern California.

Invitations for weddings at 920 Sacramento Street were highly valued, for these festivities were among the most joyful to be had. Donaldina and several of the older girls left the house early in the morning to shop at the flower market; they returned laden with arms full of white blooms. They then charged up and down the hills, traversing west across the city in a cable car. Wind whipped their faces and laughter rang in their ears, and Donaldina felt like a free-spirited girl again. Their destination was Golden Gate Park. John McLaren, the Scottish park superintendent and one of Miss Cameron's many friends, had instructed that the mission house be allowed to cut as many greens as they needed. Back at the home, these fresh branches were interwoven with the white blossoms to form an arched trellis.

Of Love and Travel and the Like

Their fresh scent blended with the tantalizing smells wafting from the kitchen.

On wedding days, Lo Mo acted as mother, father, and bridesmaid. Before the guests arrived, she changed into her wedding attire. The pink and sky-blue Chinese silk added rosiness to her luminous face. She walked down the aisle with the bride, proudly giving her away to the groom. After the ceremony, Donaldina presided as hostess at the reception. She slipped out to add special surprise touches to the waiting carriage, and then distributed small bags of rice for the guests to throw. She watched with a mother's mingled joy and nostalgic sadness as the carriage drove away with her newlywed daughter.

Donaldina Cameron had worked at the home for nine years. It seemed that everyone always needed her. The strain of responsibility pressed hard, day after day and night after night, until she was worn thin. The board decided that it was time for Lo Mo to take a break. A long break. A sabbatical. So after weeks of preparing her household for her absence, she stood at the entryway of the home, next to her luggage, surrounded by doleful faces. She said her last goodbyes–again. Two little girls were so distraught at her impending departure that she nearly reconsidered all of her carefully crafted plans. Others put on brave and cheerful faces, but quietly wondered how they would survive with Lo Mo gone for nearly a year.

Despite the difficult parting, Donaldina's eyes sparkled with anticipation. She was going to Scotland! She was going to China! And before she embarked on these adventures, she was going to Philadelphia to visit a man named Charles. For while hosting the weddings of her foster daughters, Donaldina's own happiness had been lately deepening with the hopes of a woman in love.

Donaldina traveled by train across America, her first time to see the majestically jagged Rocky Mountains, the undulating grasses of the Great Plains, the white farmhouses and red barns of the Midwest. The rhythmic clacking of the train relaxed her into uncharacteristically indulgent reveries. Her thoughts meandered to the day she had first met Charles Bazata. He was the younger brother of her sister Jesse's pastor. The Bazatas were a Czech family, full of vim. Donaldina loved their energy, which seemed even to match that of the Scottish Camerons.

Charles was a big, blond football player. He made Donaldina laugh with his spoofs, and he won her respect with his gentility. They shared the same earnest and devout faith, and both had the ability to find pleasure in a multitude of activities. They started to seek each other out whenever Donaldina visited her family. They rode horses in the hills, sang around the piano, worshipped side-by-side in church, and fell in love.

Charles moved to the opposite edge of the continent to study at New Jersey's Presbyterian seminary. They had been writing letters, and soon they would see each other again. Donaldina's heart swelled with anticipation as the train clacked to a halt in Philadelphia.

They had planned a whole week together before Donaldina's ship left for Scotland, but delays in her travels left them a mere day. Instead of the blithe times they had hoped for, the two faced the serious and daunting question of their future: Would they marry? If so, how and when? And where would they live? Donaldina did not feel free to leave her work in San Francisco, nor did Charles feel free to leave his work on the East Coast. In addition, Donaldina's three unmarried sisters would need someone to take care of them in their old age, and Charles had to support his widowed mother.

Charles and Donaldina spent the day preoccupied with their dilemma. That evening, they went to the pier where Donaldina's steamship prepared to sail. They paced back and forth on the dock as waves incessantly swooshed against the pilings. Donaldina watched her feet walk along the moist wood: right and left, right and left. It was past midnight when they abruptly ceased pacing at the bottom of the gangplank. The words said during this time have been committed to the lost annals of history that shall never be revealed, but Donaldina would confide to closest friends and family that, after hours of intense conversation, the two concluded they were not free to marry. God was calling them to lead two separate lives.

Donaldina sailed east late that night, craning her neck to watch the last shadowy strip of shoreline recede in the distance. She had said goodbye to the man she loved, fully believing that by doing so she had sacrificed any hope of matrimony.

The long, serene ocean crossing, touched with September calm, gave Donaldina time to recover from heartache and exhaustion. She sat on the deck, letting the sun wrap its warm beams around her weary body, and taking pleasure in conversation with a new friend, a fellow social reformer. They enjoyed walking the deck together with a kindly older gentleman.

After docking in Liverpool, Donaldina took the train to Inverness, Scotland. She had corresponded for years with her far-off family. Among those she had never yet met was her sister Isabella, who had been left in the care of grandparents when the rest of the family immigrated to New Zealand. Donaldina and Isabella feasted for weeks on stories, laughter, and mutual love. They tramped over purple heather-covered glens and moors, sharing decades of their lives. The Scottish wilderness resonated in Donaldina's soul. It was a relief to take deep, unhurried breaths of this fresh air after the grease and smoke of San Francisco. She was also utterly delighted at discoveries about her family: Aunt Annie was "a spinster with a great sense of humor, who lived in an adorable little stone house," and the Grand Dame Great Aunt Jess Mackenzie was pleasantly surprised to learn that her niece from the wild west of America could actually speak English quite nicely.

Fierce Compassion

After Christmas in London, Donaldina embarked on an Indian-bound voyage led by Captain Stephenson, a lifelong Cameron family friend. They were well into their trip when the captain woke Donaldina near dawn to tell her that they were passing Mount Sinai. The Captain escorted her to the deck and pointed to the mountain, then left her to experience the sight in privacy. She gazed, awestruck, while clouds slipped away and a rugged, majestic mountain appeared, gold in the light of dawn, glowing for a few seconds before a mantle of cloud shrouded it again.

In Calcutta, Donaldina visited her cousin Patrick Cameron who managed the Hong Kong and Shanghai Bank and lived with his wife Gertrude in an elegant marble home. While she was there, another cousin visited from his tea plantation, arriving on elephant. He intended to bring his American cousin on a trip to the Taj Mahal, but to her disappointment, her more sedate hosts demurred that women did not go on such exploits. The adventurous Donaldina did, however, have a good bit of fun sliding down a hill on a huge banana leaf, joining a group of children who enjoyed the novelty of a foreign woman partaking in their daily romp.

Next came China. She had heard so much about the bright green of fresh rice shoots and the beauty of small Chinese villages nestled in lush hills. She wanted to see it all. She reunited with daughters, who rejoiced to host Lo Mo in their own land. She appreciated the picturesque scenes of flooded rice fields, misty hills, thatch-roofed homes, boatmen poling upstream, children splashing in water and working in fields. Though still beset by anarchy and poverty, rural China held many gems of beauty. She understood the shock that many of her girls must have gone through when they were uprooted and transplanted to loud San Francisco with its brown mountains and cold fog.

While floating at a leisurely pace down the river on a houseboat, Donaldina relaxed in the company of her host's family. They shared this boat with their chickens, dog, and pig. The pig introduced itself to Donaldina in the twilight of a lazy evening. A snout pushed through the loose boards under her feet, tipping her off her chair and nearly tossing her backwards into the river. Her host was doubtless relieved when she responded with uproarious laughter rather than irritation.

After saying goodbye to her friend the pig, Donaldina set out for Shanghai to make one more visit to another distinguished cousin, Sir Ewen Cameron. He was an international banker who had not only been knighted by the king of England but was also the first Caucasian to be given the official title of Mandarin by the imperial Chinese government. (Sir Ewen's great-great-grandson David Cameron would be elected Prime Minister of the United Kingdom in 2010; thus is Donaldina Cameron related to the British Prime Minister.) Unfortunately, by the time Donaldina reached Shanghai, her cousin Sir Ewen was away in England. But she was given a tour of his impressive bank. She also visited schools, missions, offices, and homes to speak about the horrors she had seen in the Chinese slave trade, hoping to raise awareness and concern on the supply end of the human trafficking chain.

Nearly a year after she had left San Francisco, Donaldina's final ship passed through the headlands of the Golden Gate. She had traveled around the world and was eager to return, happy to see her California mountains welcoming her home again. As they glided into San Francisco Bay, she held on to the rail of the ship, looking fondly at the city's skyline and trying to decide which stories she would first tell her girls.

A tugboat chugged along next to the arriving steamship, carrying the officials who would take care of immigration paperwork. Donaldina's fellow passengers noticed a gigantic basket of pink roses sitting on the tugboat's dock. They were so beautiful! Whose might they be? The crowd watched curiously as a ladder was dropped from the ship to the smaller boat. Donaldina recognized one of the men on the tugboat–John Gardener, a government interpreter who often helped her in court. He picked up the basket of flowers, holding them with one hand while he carefully mounted the ladder with the other.

Fierce Compassion

Clambering onto the ship, he carved a path through the other observers and strode up to Donaldina. Handing her the basket of roses, he said, "I am the envoy of your family, but these speak their language better than I."

Donaldina knew the sacrifice the girls and staff of 920 must have made to purchase this lavish gift. She held the flowers close. She was home.

Portrait of Donaldina Cameron, 1900

Chapter Nine
Family Scrapbook

家園

*A father to the fatherless, a defender of widows,
is God in his holy dwelling.
God sets the lonely in families,
he leads forth the prisoners with singing;
but the rebellious live in a sun-scorched land.*
Psalm 68:5-6

Donaldina sat at her desk, mulling over what to write. The annual board meeting was approaching, and she needed to compile a report of the year's work. There were so many stories to be told—so many! Days and nights were jammed full of action and suspense and tales of the utmost excitement. But she should also explain the vitally important though less dramatic work of cooking, cleaning, sewing, nursing, and teaching by which former slaves gradually prepared for the rest of their lives. And she longed to communicate something of those ephemeral moments that sometimes snuck in: a jolt of joy during daily household worship or a flicker of light dawning onto a previously darkened countenance. She knew that she was surrounded by miracles as the love of God was interwoven with their daily rhythms in a way that pushed out suspicion and fear and built a band of sisters who would live and die for each other. How to capture all of this in words?

She stood up abruptly, pushed back the chair, and paced to and fro in her office. There were so many stories to be told. So many faces. So many heart-wrenching scenes. Memories spilled in.

Chow Hay: Faithful Friend

Bang, bang, bang! The urgent clamor of the knocker resonated throughout 920. "A slave girl on Stockton Street. She goes by name Chow Hay." As she heaved in gulps of air, the shaking neighbor finished, "She tried to kill herself. Drank hair dye. Soon her owner will come back and discover her."

Donaldina grabbed the telephone and rang up her friend Detective Reynolds. Two minutes later, she bolted down the hill to meet him. They climbed rickety stairs to a metal-barred door. Before Detective Reynolds could use his crowbar, a child came to the door, opened it, and then fled down the hallway and into a room. Missionary and detective were searching intently when a tiny face peered out from behind pots in a cupboard. When she saw the two white strangers, the girl screamed. The detective scooped her up over his shoulder, and she kicked and hollered the whole way up the hill back to 920, a strange sight indeed.

Donaldina smiled. Chow Hay's suicide attempt and terrified screaming contrasted so sharply with the quickly emerging, confident affection that blossomed soon after her arrival at 920. Her adoration of Lo Mo was quite evident. And yet Chow Hay had not been completely content, for there was another child slave, her dearest friend, named Quai Fah, who still suffered every day. Chow Hay spoke constantly of her friend and begged Lo Mo to find her. But Donaldina could find no trace of Quai Fah. Weeks passed without locating her.

The Lunar New Year came once more and Chinatown erupted in brilliant firecrackers and festive parades. The vigilantly protected residents of 920 ventured out to behold some of the festivities from the safety of the steps. Chow Hay was watching, delighted, as the bright blues, yellows, and greens illuminated the night sky, when suddenly her eyes widened and she gripped the arm of the interpreter, "It's Quai Fah! She is coming toward the house!"

The interpreter responded quickly, without panic. "Do not talk to her," she warned, "we will follow them and find out where she lives so that we can go there later."

Chow Hay was not quite satisfied with this answer, so she hastily and cleverly devised another solution. When Quai Fah's group was about to walk past the home, Chow Hay ran up to Lo Mo and grasped her tightly, lovingly and loudly blurting out, "Mama!" As she clung to Donaldina's skirts, she looked directly into the eyes of Quai Fah. An understanding passed between them in that glance.

That night, Lo Mo studied her maps. She had just charted out a course of action to save Quai Fah when a timid knock sounded at the door. There stood the girl–pale, thin, quivering. She had risked her life to run from the house when her mistress was gone. While Lo Mo and the interpreter were still figuring out what had happened, Chow Hay flew past in a jubilant blur to welcome her friend to 920.

That would be a good story to include in the board report. Donaldina, overcome with thankfulness, paused momentarily to jot down, "Chow Hay." Then she added: "No words can tell our gratitude to Him who gives us the happiness of having a part in His marvelous plans for saving such helpless and innocent children." Leaving the rest of Chow Hay's story to write later, she resumed pacing, as other memories tumbled over her.

Yuen Ho: Beloved Wife

Yuen Ho was happily married. Then, caught in the perilous riptides of Chinatown, she was abducted and sold. When her desperate husband tried to rescue her, he was shot and left on the street to die.

With his dwindling strength, he dragged himself to the doorstep of 920 to beg for help. Donaldina remembered the pain etched in his face as he cried out, "Oh, don't let them spoil my wife!"

And so Donaldina rescued Yuen Ho, and her husband survived the murder attempt, but just barely. He had been badly wounded, and it would take months before he recovered enough to work again. The couple lived in poverty, with a meager income from Yuen Ho's work as a seamstress. She sewed day after day, from early morning to late at night. Donaldina and staff from 920 visited them when they could, bringing gifts of food and encouragement. Donaldina sat down and wrote "Yuen Ho" on her paper. Perhaps it would be helpful for the home's supporters to read this story of marital love and perseverance in the hard, gritty environment of Chinatown.

The clanging phone interrupted Donaldina's reflections, and she talked with an immigration officer who needed housing for a woman just arrived from Hong Kong. After hanging up, she looked at the clock, realized that it was time for everyone to gather for evening prayer, and so left her scribbled notes.

Yoke Hay: Sobbing Child

Donaldina finished the evening Bible lesson and delivered dozens of good night kisses, admired one daughter's artwork and sympathized over another's cut finger, sat down to visit with three who were recovering from measles, and gave a listening ear to an older daughter's anxieties about an upcoming court date. Back in her office, Donaldina stared out the window at the lamp-lit street. A shadow crossed her face as she thought of the night activities commencing in the buildings spread out below her. Girls would be raped and beaten tonight, and not all stories ended happily ever after. She cringed as her eyes passed over the small shop filled with the plants and powders of a Chinese herbalist. Yoke Hay was just a little girl, a very little girl, who toiled day after day in the basement of this shop, splitting wood for this herbalist's cooking fire. She had been rescued, but her owner took Donaldina to court to regain custody. During the trial, the pressure of seeing her old master, and of being intently heckled by his lawyer, overwhelmed Yoke Hay. She broke down in the witness stand, contradicted herself in her testimony, and was returned to her owner. When she was thirteen, he would sell her for a good profit to a brothel, where she would most likely be kept until she died. Donaldina sighed with remorse. She had failed this girl. The desperate sound of Yoke Hay's sobs haunted her.

Mei Ling: Lonely Survivor

Mei Ling, Donaldina reasoned, would be a good example of the intense shame branded on the very souls of these girls, and how they feared the friendship and love that they most longed for.

Graceful as a river reed, lovely Mei Ling came to the home willingly, but the open, carefree relationships there contradicted everything she had ever known. She had heard the rumors that spirits haunted the mission house and that Miss Cameron tortured Chinese girls, and fear had taken deep root. The few words of Chinese that Lo Mo spoke were not enough to bridge the gap, but the other girls of 920 were able to commiserate with Mei Ling's predicament in a way that was uniquely their own. Her roommate Anna recognized the pallor of Mei Ling's face and the fearful flitting of her eyes.

"There's no reason to be afraid," Anna spoke soothingly to Mei Ling. The sound of that voice addressed to her in her own language was like a cool, trickling brook on a claustrophobic, sweltering day, but still the protective walls of doubt surrounding Mei Ling did not crumble. This was too good to be true. There must be a trick. Every other time in her life, when something seemed good, it had always resulted in nothing but lies and misery. Something here was unexplainable, and Mei Ling was terrified that what seemed so good would soon be snatched away. "We are safe here, Mei Ling," Anna continued, "I was a slave too but here I have found nothing but peace and happiness."

Mei Ling's lower lip started to quiver. Anna spoke gently, "It was bad?"

Yes, it was bad. The stories were slowly coaxed out in barely coherent phrases that surfaced from the ravaging sobs. She had been kept at the notorious "City of Pekin" on Jackson Street. One night, a customer took pity on her. He took his white handkerchief and tore it, giving her one half and telling her that he would give the other half to someone who would come and rescue her from her prison. When she saw someone holding the ripped handkerchief, she would know to run.

A few days later, when Donaldina burst through the doors, handkerchief in hand and police in tow, Mei Ling was terrified but ready. The room, full of men and women, quickly descended into chaos and she could not get to the door. As Mei Ling told the story to Anna, she closed her eyes, remembering the murky smell of cigar and sweat, the dim light of the kerosene lamps, the noises from the gambling tables, and the color of red. "The men cursed. They grabbed girls. They pushed me to a room with a secret door in the floor so they could hide me, but the door was stuck shut. They cursed and kicked. Lo Mo was coming toward us. I heard the interpreter's voice break through the noise, 'Come, Mei Ling! Come with us! We are here to help you.' I struggled. I broke free and began to run, but I could not reach them. A table crashed. The police were there. Then I was in the street with her, with–Lo Mo." Mei Ling sighed. "I want to be like the rest of you."

Donaldina dipped her pen in ink again, thinking of Mei Ling, and wrote, "How the very deep heart hunger and need of these friendless Chinese girls appeals to our sympathies! When in their hour of loneliness and distress they turn to us for comfort and guidance in the serious problems of their lives, how great a joy and privilege is ours to be able to help even a very little!"

Family Scrapbook

Flora Wong: Devoted Sister

Edna and Flora Wong's parents were estranged. The court designated their mother as their legal guardian, but their father, furious about this judgment, took them by force. Shortly afterwards, he ran off in a crazed state, leaving the sisters abandoned. A little while after their father disappeared, Flora was found and taken to 920, but the younger girl, Edna, had been separated from her sister and sold. Flora felt responsible for her lost sister and grieved every day. The home searched, in vain. Finally, after eight years, a rumor hinted that Edna might be in Victoria, British Columbia. Donaldina undertook this trip with Flora. The hopeful quest ended next to the little grave where Edna was buried. Donaldina's acute memory of this sight inspired her pen, as she wrote that "No words can describe the pathos of a sister's helpless sorrow as the bitter tears of regret and pity fell fast over that silent, yet eloquent earth mound where her dearest hope lay buried." Donaldina had introduced Flora Wong to the board in an earlier report; now she should share the sad ending.

Old Sam: One Story for a Slave Owner

A smile crossed Donaldina's face at the thought of Old Sam. The story was longer and more complex than some of the others, but it was certainly one that the board would greatly appreciate.

Several years ago, Donaldina had traveled by train to Marysville, over a hundred miles northeast of San Francisco, to answer a rescue plea. She set out at dusk, after securing a hotel room and a young police officer. They found the girl sitting in a miserable heap in the corner of a shack, waiting to be called on by the men who played their game of cards in the center of the room. But tonight, she was also hoping that the woman named Lo Mo would appear. The moment she spotted a white woman with a police officer, she jumped up. They stealthily slipped out before the men realized what was happening. All was well. Rescue missions were rarely so easy.

Back at the hotel, Donaldina noticed that the girl was wearing the flimsiest of silk clothing. A bundle of warmer clothes had been left behind in the rush of the escape. The frigid night air had already pinched her cheeks raw and red. Donaldina had no extra clothes. There was certainly no place to buy them in the middle of the night, and they were due to catch the early morning train back to San Francisco. Donaldina saw only one option. "Stay right here in the room," Donaldina told the girl, "and open the door to no one."

The obliging policeman had returned to the station and was contentedly sitting out the duration of his shift when Miss Cameron walked through the door and requested that he assist her once more. He was understandably aghast when he heard that she was going back for a bag of clothes, but she persuaded him. Retracing their steps, they found the sagging door ajar, and they snuck back in, finding the clothes exactly where the girl had said they were. Donaldina grabbed them and turned around–right into a very large and livid man who blocked the doorway and loudly demanded the return of his property. The police officer tackled him to let Donaldina through. She started out the door, but heard a scuffle and turned back. The man had a gun. Donaldina rushed into the fray. In a second, the revolver was in the officer's hands and handcuffs were on the assailant's wrists. Donaldina scooped up the bundle of clothing and paraded out with the policeman and the big, cursing, handcuffed slave owner.

Donaldina loved this story because of its surprise ending. The slave owner, nicknamed Old Sam, was so impressed by the events of that night that he decided to abandon his illegal business. He asked an attorney if Miss Cameron would interfere if he tried to bring his legitimate wife from China. The attorney assured him that Miss Cameron was only interested in rescuing illegally held slaves, and would have no claim on his lawful wife. Relieved, Old Sam prepared to sail for China. But first, he would visit the woman who had barged into his business, stolen his slave girl, and precipitated his arrest. So

Family Scrapbook

Old Sam sat down for tea with Miss Cameron, and she wished him all happiness in his reunion with his wife.

Donaldina with her girls

The Keeper of the Scrapbook

Discouragement, sorrow, rage, surprise, laughter, joy–Donaldina knew them all in full measure. Her days overflowed with work, some dramatic and some mundane. She taught her daughters the Bible and administered their classrooms. She supervised menus and chores. She interacted with board members and visitors. She collaborated with police officers, immigration officials, judges, and lawyers who came to her with questions and problems regarding their work with the Chinese. She was recognized in the San Francisco courthouse, where she repeatedly appeared to appeal for the welfare of her girls. Many in San Francisco and the rest of California greatly admired the superintendent of the house on the hill. Others thought she was meddlesome, aand resented her for overstepping the traditional bounds of a female social service worker.

She had not yet written about the babies. Born sometimes to free women and sometimes to slaves, they were sometimes at risk of being snatched away and sold; loving mothers brought them to the home for protection. Nor had she explained the boys who were occasionally brought to them. Oh, it would be good to have a separate home for the smallest girls, and another for the boys. And then there was the new work among Japanese women…

As Donaldina continued to ponder how she should best speak on behalf of all of those under her care, she thought gratefully of Jesus. It was his love that called forth this work. He was her strength in need, counselor in perplexity, comfort in sorrow, and companion in joy.

The house was finally quiet. Donaldina stopped pacing. She sat down at the desk once more, dipped nib in ink, and began to write:

With the past year literally crammed full of rescue work, with all that it implies of struggle, victory and defeat, sorrow of the deepest, joy of the fullest, it is difficult to write an annual message for our friends that will convey in the smallest measure to their minds what has really taken place here in your Presbyterian Mission Home… Nor can one begin to convey to the minds of our readers in this limited space an adequate idea of the varied appeals which come to us daily all through the year from without, and hourly from within, asking help, advice, sympathy, and guidance… We find it difficult to condense into anything like a brief report what has taken place during the year. In work like ours there is so much–in a way the most vital part of the work is chronicled only in our hearts.

Chapter Ten
Though the Earth Give Way

拯救

*The days passed quickly, happily, calmly.
No premonition crossed the mind of anyone in that busy, hopeful household
that we were preparing our dear old home for its burial.*
Donaldina Cameron

*Therefore we will not fear, though the earth give way
and the mountains fall into the heart of the sea.*
Psalm 46:2

The year was 1906 and San Francisco had shaken off the stigma of bubonic plague. Boardwalks had been replaced with concrete sidewalks to discourage rodents, and rotting buildings were exchanged with the new and modern. The hilly peninsula that had once been a wild gold rush outpost was now the ninth largest city in the United States, proudly dubbed the "Gateway to the Pacific." Musicians, artists, and tourists came from all over the country and the world. San Francisco was stylish, optimistic, and pleased with itself.

Some experts in the growing science of seismology warned that San Francisco might be shaken with a large earthquake. But no one worried much.

It was the evening of April 17, 1906. Donaldina took one last look over the meeting hall. It shimmered and shone, with not a speck of dust to be seen. Normal routines that day had been relaxed as everyone vigorously scoured the house from top to bottom and prepared final details of performances and hospitality. Tomorrow was the Mission Home's annual meeting, a highlight of each year. Board members came together to hear stories from the past and plan for the future, while they also enjoyed time to talk with the girls and admire their performances.

Donaldina climbed the stairs and stepped into her room. It was late and she was tired. She slipped off her shoes and felt her body slowly relax. Tomorrow would be a good day.

5:00 a.m. All are sleeping. Sacramento Street is silent.

5:05. A single bird sings a strain of song. The grey of dawn is just beginning to touch darkened Chinatown, and the shape of the bay gradually emerges in the early morning light.

5:10. A stray cat slinks past the home. A man comes out of an apartment door and walks down Sacramento Street on the way to his job at a grocery market.

5:12. A terrific noise shatters the tranquil silence. The bird stops its song. The cat is buried under bricks. The man walking down Sacramento Street is hurled to the ground. The bells of St. Mary's church start to clang crazily.

Donaldina Cameron catapulted from her bed into an oncoming dresser. Her eyes flew open in confusion. What was this? Had the home been attacked? Was this the time for the end of the world? All she knew was that she must get to her girls. Confused, half-awake, they were already streaming out of their rooms. Donaldina was with them in a minute, and opened her mouth to take command of the situation, but then stood transfixed as she watched the scene unfold. Her heart rejoiced. As plaster fell in chunks onto the floor, her daughters were quietly helping each other. Older girls did not show their fear; they soothed the little ones. They picked each other up, held each other's hands, stayed steady while the floor trembled. Donaldina glowed with pride at the unselfish courage of her daughters.

Mrs. Browne had spent the night at the house in preparation for the meeting the next day, and Donaldina was immensely grateful to have her. They counted staff and residents and, greatly relieved, thanked God that all were safe. Then they surveyed the damage: the building stood, but the chimney had collapsed, so they could not cook. Older girls calmed the younger ones and helped them dress, while the housekeeper managed to procure a large basket of bread from a nearby bakery. This and some apples made their breakfast, which was "the last meal eaten in the hospitable dining-room of 920. Our girls gathered round the little white tables, sang as usual the morning hymn, then repeated the Twenty-third Psalm with more feeling and a deeper realization of its unfailing promises than ever before."

While eating, they were startled by an aftershock. Dishes rattled and wide-eyed girls took hold of each other's hands. When it finished, Donaldina went upstairs to look out a window toward the city. Piles of wood and brick lay in heaps where buildings had once stood. Smoke rose from the debris, so thick in some places that it obscured the water of the bay. Later she would learn that the earthquake had ruptured the gas main, creating fires all over San Francisco. It also damaged the water mains, making the fires difficult to extinguish. As she looked down at rubble and smoke, Donaldina heard horse hooves and watched the United States Calvary gallop by: the mayor had called for troops to prevent looting. A menacing dread had gripped the city.

Three dedicated board members, concerned about what the earthquake might have done to 920, walked to the home to help. They discussed how to protect the large family, finally deciding to walk west, away from the worst fires, to seek shelter in the Presbyterian Church on Van Ness Street about a mile away.

Once the decision was made, action was quick. Donaldina wanted to make sure her girls would not be out after nightfall. She recognized tong members milling around with the crowds that were moving up the hill to flee fires, and she knew that some would take advantage of the chaos to try to snatch girls and women. Everyone was put to work collecting bedding, food, and clothing, as much as they could carry; then they assembled outside the home, where Donaldina counted and organized their band.

"Looking Down Sacramento Street, 1906" by Arnold Genthe, taken as San Franciscans fled uphill from the growing fire below. 920 Sacramento is the third building down on the left side of the street.

Though the Earth Give Way

Teens and young women carried the youngest children, and the small girls toted parcels. They tramped up Nob Hill, joining others who were fleeing the lower parts of town. The group's three babies included a newborn whose mother, a recently rescued slave, was too feeble to help. The strong helped the weak, and they encouraged each other on. It was a frightening, arduous afternoon, and none would ever forget the flight "through intense heat and suffocating smoke, toiling over the steepest hills, encumbered by all manner of burdens and weighed down by intense anxiety for the safety of the many little children and others in our care."

When they reached their destination, everyone settled down on pew cushions in the basement of the church, hoping for sleep after a very long day. Then Donaldina realized her mistake. Her hand flew to her mouth. She had left all of her precious guardianship papers at 920. If those were lost or destroyed, slave owners would challenge her in court, and they might win. It would only be a matter of weeks, maybe even days, before they swarmed to the courthouses to see how many girls they could claim. Donaldina saw only one course of action. She must go back through rubble and fire to the house. She must have those papers.

Leaving her girls sleeping, Donaldina stepped back into the haunted streets, which were dark but for the eerie glow of fire. As she retraced her steps, all was shadowed, including the troops who guarded against curfew-breaking looters. They challenged her, but she persuaded them to let her continue. Smoke choked her as she neared Chinatown. When she reached Powell Street, she was relieved that her home still stood. She rushed down the last half block and started up the stairs, when she was stopped by an authoritative "Halt!" She turned around and faced a soldier.

"You can't go in."

"I am Miss Cameron."

"You can't go in!"

Fierce Compassion

"This is the Mission Home for rescued slave girls. I am its director. I must get my girls' legal papers."

The soldier raised his gun: "I have orders to shoot anyone who tries to enter a building."

"Shoot then!" She ran up the stairs and through the door while the shouts of the soldier followed her through the building.

Donaldina surveyed her office by the light of the fire outside. Memories of the past eleven years rushed back to her as she laid hold of the papers and a few small valuables. An explosion rocked the building, and plaster and glass shattered to the floor around her. The soldier yelled at her to get out. The fire department was dynamiting parts of Chinatown in an attempt to create a firebreak that would protect the wealthy neighborhoods further up the hill. They were very near now. Donaldina snatched the big black ledger and rushed out, taking a last look at the rooms so dear to her. She whispered, "Good night, dear home," and sped into the street. Soon after she left, dynamite was laid at the steps of 920 Sacramento Street and the beloved building was obliterated.

Donaldina's day had begun at 5:12 am. By the time she reached her daughters back at the church, it was nearly dawn again. While lying down for a brief rest, she brainstormed possible plans of action. It would be best to get out of the city and across the bay. If they could

920 after being dynamited

find a ferry, they could head north to San Anselmo and perhaps stay with friends at the San Francisco Theological Seminary.

"Lo Mo?" A little face peered out at Donaldina. Early morning light cast fuzzy shadows on the walls. "What are we going to do today? Will we stay here? Can we go back to our home? Please? I left my favorite dress there and I want to go and get it."

Groggily, Donaldina opened her eyes. Her heart lurched as she remembered the now demolished 920. "No, child, we can't go back to the home."

The girls stirred and questions were soon coming at Donaldina from every corner of the room. Donaldina mustered her energy, sat up, and cleared her throat, "Hold on one moment, girls. Your questions will be answered for you as the day plays out. For now just wash up as best you can and we will have prayer before we prepare for another walk."

Hours of preparation ensued. They could only take what they could carry, and today's walk would be longer than yesterday's. Some of the girls tore up sheets to make bundles, creatively attaching them to broom handles so that they could carry two loads, vegetable-peddler style, across their shoulders. By the time Donaldina and her troop emerged from the church, the sun was high. It was an odd-looking sun, filtered through smoke and dust to reveal strangely shaped piles of rubble and disoriented, wandering people. The motley group of girls and women began another trek, now walking in the direction of the thickest smoke and fire. A few other displaced Chinatown stragglers, not knowing what else to do, joined them, until they had a parade of nearly seventy.

Donaldina rallied the morale of her fatigued group. She smiled tenderly at a fragile five-year-old who tearfully agreed to carry two-dozen eggs when told that she might be able to eat some of them later. She offered indulgent sympathy to the young lady heavily laden with the large box of letters from her devoted suitor. She pointed out the courage of Old Sing Ho, half blind, who managed the walk by rolling the bag that carried all her possessions down the hills and then cheerfully dragging it back up. Donaldina also comforted Yuen Kum, who was engaged to be married on April 21, just three days away. Her fiancé was traveling from Cleveland for the wedding. How would he ever find his bride? Though prospects were grim at best, love sustained them, and "laughter was the tonic which stimulated that weary, unwashed, and uncombed procession on the long tramp through stifling, crowded streets near where the fire raged."

The dust-filtered sun was setting when the ragged group reached the end of Market Street and found a ferry that would take them north to Sausalito. They dropped their bundles gratefully on the floor and sank down on top of them. Donaldina gazed over her flock, exhausted but inexpressibly thankful.

Friends at the seminary received them gladly, though all they could offer for housing was an old barn. The large family happily accepted this temporary home and camped there for weeks. They slept on straw and ate multitudes of boiled red beans, taking turns with their small supply of silverware and plates.

In their turmoil of homelessness, the household celebrated a magnificent event together. The bridegroom found his bride! He had arrived in burning San Francisco on the day of the earthquake. He had no inkling as to the whereabouts of his bride, but was determined to find her, though San Francisco was burned down and all was in chaos. And so he did. Three days after the quake, on the originally planned date of April 21, a wedding took place in the seminary's ivy-covered chapel, nestled picturesquely at the base of a mountain. Donaldina breathed a sigh of happiness and relief. This man had proven himself and would surely care for his wife.

Months later, Lo Mo smiled, remembering this wedding as she finished writing her account of the earthquake for the mission house board:

Notwithstanding all the difficulties the young man had gone through in finding his fiancée...and all the trying experiences through which Yuen Kum had passed, they were a happy couple as they received the congratulations of those present. Just after the wedding, Mr. and Mrs. Henry Lai started for their home in Cleveland amidst showers of California roses and the best wishes of their many friends. So romance with its magic touch helped us for a time to forget our great losses.

The San Francisco earthquake was felt from Oregon to Los Angeles and is considered to be one of the worst natural disasters in United States history. Attempts to create firebreaks by dynamiting buildings went awry. Mayor Schmitz, fearful of looting, widely publicized his order that soldiers and police shoot anyone entering a demolished building. Hundreds were shot.

Because Chinatown residents were put in a refugee camp and not permitted to return to their homes, thousands of fortune hunters descended on Chinatown to take what they could. Army officials allowed looting in Chinatown to run rampant; some even participated. On the third day after the earthquake, the Chinese consul general lodged a protest with California governor George Pardee, complaining that the National Guard was stripping everything of value in Chinatown. Accounts of the time indicate that Chinatown looters included some of the most prominent citizens of the Bay area.

It took four days and nights to put out the fires, leaving about eighty percent of San Francisco destroyed. More than half the people in the city were homeless and many would live in refugee camps for two years.

But San Francisco was ever-optimistic. Five days after the earthquake, Governor Pardee declared confidently that "the work of rebuilding San Francisco has commenced, and I expect to see the great metropolis replaced on a much grander scale than ever before." When he made this proclamation, his thoughts of San Francisco's great metropolis probably did not include a house for slave survivors and orphans in Chinatown. But this beloved home also would be rebuilt.

Chapter Eleven
The New 920

堅忍

*A bruised reed he will not break,
and a smoldering wick he will not snuff out.
In faithfulness he will bring forth justice;
he will not falter or be discouraged
till he establishes justice on earth.*
Isaiah 42:3-4

"Lo Mo! What happened to the bricks? They look funny." A sweet little face peered curiously at the awkwardly protruding shapes.

"Oh, yes, my dear. Aren't they so interesting? These are very special bricks. They survived the earthquake and fire, just like us. They started melting from the terrible heat, but then they cooled into these new shapes, and now they are perfectly fitted together to build strong walls for our new home." As Donaldina admired the newly built 920 Sacramento with one of her littlest daughters, she mused over the fact that the people who lived on the inside of this building were akin to these clinker bricks on the outside: each had undergone trauma and been re-formed; each was now uniquely shaped and had been placed together perfectly with the others to make their strong family refuge.

Fierce Compassion

Donaldina touched one of the bricks just as the sun broke through clouds. It was April 14, 1908. Almost exactly two years after the earthquake, friends gathered to celebrate the dedication of the New 920. The messenger boy arrived on his bicycle early that morning, bringing the first of many telegrams of love and encouragement from around the country.

Donaldina greeted guests with a smile and ushered them on tours of the new building. Meanwhile, her mind wandered back over the past two years. The 920 family (minus the 920 part, that is) had lived as refugees, traipsing around San Anselmo and Oakland, filling any accommodation that could possibly be found for a household of some fifty girls and women. First, it was the big, drafty barn. She remembered her excruciating exhaustion those nights as her ragged girls, reeking of smoke, settled down to sleep. Just as the excitement of camping in a barn was beginning to wear thin, Donaldina gratefully accepted the offer of a nearby house. A real house, big enough for all of them, at the end of a long drive and surrounded by hawthorn and acacia trees–to Lo Mo and her girls, it looked like a fairy palace.

Though they had been very thankful for this home, life still felt transitional and temporary. Donaldina sometimes thought wistfully of precious treasures that had burned in the fire: letters from family and friends, souvenirs from her sabbatical, her favorite hats and scarves. But they must move forward now. The household maximized use of every available resource and improvised creative solutions as needed. When someone donated a large, tent-like canvas, they set it up in the yard as a makeshift schoolhouse.

Though this new home was charming, it was not very secure. One day, someone spotted familiar tong men walking near the house. Most likely they were scoping out the situation in hopes of snatching girls from Fahn Quai. Everyone was put on alert and warned not to wander off.

One afternoon, girls playing in the yard were alarmed by a suspicious scuffling noise on the other side of the stone wall. They ran inside to tell Lo Mo, who dropped what she was doing and hurried out. Wide-eyed girls pointed to where they had heard the ominous sounds. Donaldina grimly strode in that direction. She picked up a rock, dug her shoes into cracks in the wall, and climbed to the top. With one hand, she held on to the wall. With her other hand, she hurled the rock over the top. It fell with a clunk—onto the back of an unsuspecting cow.

The cow made for a funny story, but the insecurity of living in such an open, unprotected setting needed to change. San Francisco was still digging out of rubble; moving back now was impossible. So they crossed the bay again and looked for a home in Oakland. Donaldina talked with many landlords who were unwilling to a take a large household of Chinese orphans and former prostitutes. Finally, they found a place, which quickly became too small, and then another that would suffice. In Oakland, a thriving slave network again surrounded them, and Donaldina again felt the daily strain of protecting her flock. She forged new relationships with local law enforcement, and the Oakland police quickly came to value the ally they had in Miss Cameron. They asked her to participate in slave raids, and more residents were added to the ranks of the 920 nomads. More people to help, more people to love. They healed, studied, worked. Some travelled back to China to reunite with their families. Life returned to a relative state of normalcy, though with the additional inconveniences and insecurities of refugees. Resolve to return to Sacramento Street was strong. A campaign raised funds for a new mission home and donations came from around the country.

When the time came to design the new building, Donaldina asked for a home-like atmosphere, an appealing, approachable sort of place. A roomy parlor with fireplace around which they could gather would be lovely. She was disappointed to discover that the architect was not concerned with a homey ambience. His top priorities were to maximize the limited building materials available during San Francisco's post-fire building rush and to build a practical, strong structure capable of housing a large number of orphans. The result was a solid cube of a building, without any chummy hearthside parlor.

Still, it would be wonderful to be back home on Sacramento Street. The family planned to move into the New 920 several weeks before its official dedication day. Donaldina herded her entourage onto streetcars and ferry for the last ride of their post-earthquake pilgrimage. Sunlight bouncing off the bay dazzled their eyes and wind spattered their cheeks with droplets of salty water. The eclectic group stepped back into San Francisco and maneuvered away from the ferry building and financial district into Chinatown. New buildings with bright red pagoda roofs lined Grant Avenue–the rebuilding of Chinatown had been undertaken with tourism in mind. Finally, the procession of girls and women trooped up the hill and to the home that awaited their arrival. One of the younger girls ran up to Donaldina and reached for her hand. "You're like Moses, aren't you Lo Mo? Leading us to the Promised Land."

Promised Land? Hiding places in Chinatown still harbored violent crime. Human beings were still bought and sold behind bolted doors. Tongs still ruled by terror. Grinding hardship and desolate loneliness still drove men to wreck their health and finances in dark rooms filled with opium and gambling; brutal prostitution still destroyed the lives of hundreds of women. Perhaps the memories of these shadows darkened the minds of some of the teenagers and women. But dreadful thoughts did not seem to cloud the young girls' happiness. Gleeful shouts resonated as they ran across the threshold of their home. Girls ran upstairs, girls ran downstairs; they staked their claims on bedrooms; they explored every hidden hallway and cleaning closet with the utmost excitement.

Several weeks later, at the home's dedication, Chinese and American guests gave inspiring speeches. A poem of consecration was read in Chinese and translated into English. Donaldina listened as her thoughts wandered through the memories of the past two years. "Miss Cameron," a voice sliced through her contemplation, "would you make some remarks for us?"

Donaldina looked over the gathered group and smiled. She told the story of their pilgrimage over the past two years, and the telling turned into an overflow of thankfulness. "As we begin to enumerate our blessings, they appear to multiply." She paused and reflected for a moment before resoundingly declaring that, "There are so many bright and hopeful things in this work, we should never be discouraged. With God all things are possible."

Here she was, surrounded by a large, devoted family, many of whom had survived rejection and abuse as well as earthquake and fire. People remade. A home remade. Gratitude overwhelmed her, and joyful tears illuminated her eyes as the group began to sing one of her favorite hymns. Tone-deaf Donaldina joined in heartily:

> Granting the sinner life and peace,
> Granting the captive sweet release,
> Shedding His blood to make us free,
> Merciful Man of Calvary!

The celebratory atmosphere was soon set aside for the hard work of daily living. Donaldina's journal from that time shows her capacity to see and enjoy the "bright, beautiful" things in her life. But sometimes, it also reveals fatigued discouragement:

> *A cold showery day. Mrs. Sing of Los Angeles came to see Margaret. Dr. Muller called. Mrs. Newhall, Mr. Chesney called. Wing and his friend called. Ah Tye & Miss C took N'Gun Que to get her things on Spofford Alley. Had Chinese lunch with Mrs. Sing and the girls. Lai Kum and Jim met here to discuss their plans. Bok Yan called. Man to see N'Gun Que. A busy rather profitless day.*

Fierce Compassion

Buried under many responsibilities, Donaldina neglected her health. Occasionally, a pounding headache forced her to bed early. Her heart had been fluttering oddly lately; the doctor insisted on checking her when he visited a sick girl, and warned that her blood pressure was high; her tooth ached and she had put off going to the dentist.

Girls learned to recognize when Lo Mo felt strained; her playfulness turned terse and she started sentences with "My dear girls..." So many people depended on her, and she was haunted by the hidden, voiceless ones who were still tormented, night after night, their young lives plundered. Recently she had been thwarted in a rescue. She had glimpsed the slave she sought looking out at her through a window. Then the young slave vanished, jerked away and out of sight. The rescue attempt failed. Later, Donaldina heard that the slave had been beaten to death in front of others, an example to anyone else who might attempt to run away. The horrific scene replayed over and over in her mind.

Sometimes days seemed dark and fruitless. Many shared in her work, but she bore much alone, with only God hearing her anxiety and grief. Donaldina pushed through her exhaustion. It was not yet time to rest.

In the year after moving, the home was visited by outrageous fevers, aching muscles, and bulbous swelling in the girls' cheeks: the mumps. The mumps brought along their friend the measles and together the two wreaked miserable havoc. Lo Mo battled in the trenches, mopping feverish heads, changing bedding, staying up at night to console moaning patients. Then, when mumps and measles were finally quelled, sore throats arrived to prolong the agony. The doctor confirmed Donaldina's suspicion of scarlet fever.

The Board of Health quarantined the home. It was converted into a makeshift hospital, with Lo Mo as head matron–until she herself went down with scarlet fever. She hid it as long as possible, but finally the doctor commanded her to go to bed. She did manage to take fourteen calls from her sickbed that day, and write a letter on behalf of little Mah Ho Ti. After three days of imprisonment in bed she declared herself well enough to get up. Eighteen girls had the fever. Donaldina worked through the valleys of illness until they were all well and able to venture out into the fresh air again.

While the mission house fought the mumps and measles, a small cluster of buildings was being built on Angel Island, next to Alcatraz Island in San Francisco Bay. Angel Island became the Ellis Island of the West Coast, the point of entry for all immigrants coming to San Francisco. The United States was intent on stemming a dreaded tidal wave of illegal Chinese immigration.

The Chinese empire was collapsing. America still beckoned as a way out, even despite the restrictions and racism that continued to make life on the Gold Mountain so difficult. Chinese still tried to get in, even when it seemed they were not wanted. Discriminatory laws did not allow Chinese immigrants to become U.S. citizens. The exception: Those born in the United States were automatically American citizens—and so were their children, wherever their place of birth.

Most of the city's birth records were burned in the earthquake fires. Some aspiring immigrants and entrepreneurs saw this disappearance of government documents as a golden opportunity: Now, anyone could say that he was born in California. A man who claimed to be a U.S. citizen could then bring from China his sons and daughters, also citizens. If he had no children, many others were glad to pay him to pretend that he did. All these "paper sons" needed to do was convince immigration officials of their false family identity.

The compound on the rocky shore of Angel Island opened in 1910. A dormitory was surrounded by barbed wire fence. Men, women, and children were detained here while they waited for the approval or denial of their request for entry into the United States. The majority of these waiting immigrants were Chinese. Sometimes they were held for weeks, months, or even years in crowded, unsanitary conditions, not knowing how long they would stay, and not knowing whether they would be deported to China at the end of their ordeal. They were subjected to interrogations that could last for hours, intense mind games in which they were assumed guilty until they could prove themselves innocent. The immigration station on Angel Island quickly filled with fear, depression, and shame. Later, a federal investigation revealed a rampant worldwide network of corruption in the business of Chinese immigration to America. Collusions between Chinese smugglers and Caucasian officials made a money-making operation out of the vulnerable hopes of thousands. If you could not pay, you would likely be stranded on Angel Island, and finally deported back to China.

Some Angel Island inmates expressed the anguish of their detainment by writing or carving poetry on the walls next to their bunks. These poetic expressions, painstakingly written in Chinese calligraphy, speak poignant witness to the dreams of Chinese who came hoping for life in America:

> America has power, but not justice.
> In prison, we were victimized as if we were guilty.
> Given no opportunity to explain, it was really brutal.
> I bow my head in reflection but there is
> Nothing I can do.

The 920 household buzzed with excitement the day that they sent their very own Tye Leung to work at Angel Island. Tye had come to the mission home when she was twelve years old trying to escape from an arranged marriage to an older man in Montana. Ten years later, Donaldina depended on Tye as an interpreter, a singer in the quartet that represented the house, and the thrifty manager of the kitchen's menu. But Lo Mo was willing to share her for another important assignment: Tye had been given the distinction of being the first Chinese employee of the U.S. government. She would be an interpreter at the new Angel Island Immigration Station, where she would be in a wonderful position to help and encourage the confused, frightened, friendless women who were detained on the Island. The 920 household was excited at the prospect of all the good that Tye might be able to do at Angel Island.

Tye, however, did not stay at Angel Island for long. In an unexpected twist, she fell in love with an immigration official, Charles Schulze, and he with her. He was Caucasian. She was Chinese. By all societal norms, they ought not marry. Law, families, and popular culture prohibited it. But they went to Vancouver and were legally wed. When they returned to San Francisco, disapproval of their interracial marriage forced both of them to resign from their jobs at Angel Island.

Tye and Charles persevered in a long, successful marriage, raising four children and humbly serving the communities that found them so scandalous. In 1912, just after California granted women the right to vote, Tye Leung Schulze took another bold step: she became the first Chinese woman to cast a ballot in a U.S. presidential race.

After meetings in Los Angeles, Donaldina visited her brother on his ranch. As they sat in his kitchen, Allan listened, riveted, while his little sister Dolly shared her stories. Even the scarlet fever had elements of drama and humor when she told it.

A peaceful silence filled the kitchen before Donaldina changed the course of the conversation, "I saw the Tookers again in Los Angeles. They came all the way from New Jersey. Mary and Gertrude and their widowed father Nathaniel. Such a faithful, devoted family. They have shown interest in our work for several years now, and have invited me to the East Coast to speak to groups there about the important issues of Chinese slavery. I am sure you would enjoy them, Allan."

"I should be delighted to make their acquaintance," replied her brother as he rose to pour her some tea from the burbling pot on the stove.

"On the last day of the convention, I was scheduled to speak at a banquet that Mr. Tooker was also attending. I was much engrossed in conversation with the welfare worker next to me, quite the fascinating person, when I noticed that the banquet hall had become hushed. I turned to Mr. Tooker and whispered, 'What is everybody waiting for?'

"'Why for you to speak, of course!' said he. Somehow, in the midst of my engaging conversation, I failed to hear the toastmaster introduce me to the crowd."

Allan's deep laugh reverberated through the house, "I am sure that you charmed your audience nonetheless."

Once again, a brief respite with her brother's family refreshed Donaldina for the return to her arduous work. Three weeks later, on a bright, beautiful day, Donaldina stepped lightly out the door. She was on her way to the train station to meet the Tookers, who had come to San Francisco for a visit. Earthquake had not destroyed her work, nor opposition, nor illness, and her life was rich with friends and family.

The New 920 with the girls standing by the door. The same building stands today.

Chapter Twelve
Nathaniel

信仰

Dear refuge of my weary soul,
On thee, when sorrows rise,
On thee, when waves of trouble roll,
My fainting hope relies.

To Thee I tell each rising grief,
For Thou alone canst heal.
Thy Word can bring a sweet relief,
For every pain I feel.
Anne Steele

"Sue Mui had a good life in China. Her family cared for her and she was educated and accomplished in many areas." Donaldina stood erect at the podium. A white collar peeked out from the grey-blue suit that made her eyes sparkle, and an elegant hat gracefully framed her face. Her auburn hair had changed color and was now quite white, though at the age of forty her features were still young and fresh. Not a single sound from the large room competed with her confident, lilting voice. "Sue Mui was kidnapped by a highbinder from a gang that hails from this city. They disguised her in men's clothing and carried her aboard the *Manchuria*, with the darkness of the night concealing their covert deeds. She travelled across the Pacific Ocean stowed away in the lowest hold."

The speaker paused to smile ever so slightly at the jovial yet dignified face of Nathaniel Tooker, who sat in the front row; then she continued her story, "Upon arrival in San Francisco, Sue Mui was lowered into a small lifeboat during the darkest hour of the night, and she was rowed ashore. She was starting to comprehend her fate and begged to be spared, but in vain. That very night she would be sold for the price of three thousand and three hundred dollars. It seemed that her happy life was over.

"Sue Mui's family in China was frantic. Thankfully, the Mission Home has friends spread across China, as well as America, and her parents were able to contact us. She was rescued in February and is recovering quite well. Soon she will return to her family in Canton, accompanied by a missionary who will protect her from being recaptured.

"Many and varied are the experiences of even one month at the Chinese Mission Home. The sum total of twelve months would fill a book, and it would not be dull reading, not one page of it. If the girls who entered the home last year should all file past you in actual review, as they do before my mental vision, and if I could conjure up for you their pathetic and tragic histories, you would be touched with a deep pity.

"Here they come, up the steep ascent to the Haven on the Hill, a sad little procession, all ages, from dear baby Ah Que in her little mother's arms up to poor old Lee Shee, just over from China to end her days with her only son, and immediately ordered deported by our inexorable Chinese Exclusion Laws. Such heartaches you will find in this little throng, knocking for admission at the door of 920, and such peculiarities of character, such different expressions. Some young and very pretty when the traces of tears are washed away and the lines of trouble and suffering smoothed out. Some lovable and intelligent, quickly responsive, others dull and repellant. Some trustful and easily guided, others suspicious, with a deep stubbornness bred of gross ignorance and superstitious fear. All, each and every one, driven to the shelter of our home by some deep vital need, such are the ones who seek us and whom we are here to help as best we may."

Donaldina inhaled deeply and stood slightly taller before diving into the more controversial part of her speech. She briefly explained how U.S. immigration law discouraged normal family life and made the problem of Chinese slavery radically worse. Then she made an appeal to her audience, which on this particular occasion included a number of prominent men. She implored them to use their influence to change the laws that discriminated against Chinese immigration. Some raised their eyebrows. Women were not expected to so freely dispense political and legal advice. Managing an orphan girls' home was appropriate, but some thought that Miss Cameron ought not interfere in complicated matters of politics and law.

Donaldina's conclusion brought more discomfort. "Some of you have not feared to sink the best of your intellect, your time, and your talent into the development of this mission. And is it not repaying you a hundred fold year by year? I make an appeal today to those who are merely interested onlookers. Cease to stand without. Come closer; step within the circle; form another link in the magic golden chain of his love which is fast drawing together all nations."

Although some squirmed with this exhortation, others were inspired. Donaldina's impassioned voice resonated in the rafters, "Our talents are diverse, our opportunities differ, our pathways in life diverge, but our Master's call to service is the same to all. All fields are his and the promise is unfailing as the command is explicit."

After she finished, Donaldina glimpsed Nathaniel beaming at her through the crowd. He waited on the edge of the group that had gathered for a turn to speak with her. Finally the others dispersed and Nathaniel emphatically delivered his warm commendation, "Miss Cameron, that was an excellent speech!"

Donaldina's next set of speaking engagements put her on a train for a cross-country trip. Before her departure, her sister Jessie managed to snatch her for an afternoon. "Dolly!" she exclaimed, "I will not have you go gallivanting about in New York without a decent outfit. We are going to Union Square and I am buying you a new dress." Donaldina protested, but her sister had her way, and a few days later, when Donaldina rumbled down the hill in a cable car, bound for the train depot, her suitcase held a new, lovely, light blue dress the color of a spring morning sky.

In New York, Donaldina spent much of her time with her hosts, Nathaniel and his adult daughters Mary and Gertrude. She had stayed at their home before, and was relaxed and happy there. Conversations with the family and their friends were lively and stimulating, carrying on for hours into the night.

After one of Donaldina's speaking events, she and the Tooker daughters had a jolly time chatting as the mild autumnal evening turned into night. Nathaniel drove his car carefully up the ramp and onto the ferry for the return home. After the boat pulled away from the dock, he gently took Donaldina's arm and they stepped out onto the deck. Waves lapped. Reflected bits of starlight twinkled in the water. And Nathaniel asked Donaldina to marry him.

Donaldina responded quietly, lost in thought and memory. Nathaniel's proposal did not come as a great surprise. She regarded him highly, and had recognized his gradually growing affection for her. There was a time not long ago when she had been convinced that matrimony was not the path she was destined to take. Indeed, she had turned down other suitors. This time, she wanted to say yes. Nathaniel was a good man, strong in faith, affable and gentlemanly. His daughters were good friends to her. She greatly enjoyed his presence, and the prospect of life together with him was very appealing. Of course, her most worrisome concern was that Nathaniel's home was on the East Coast. She could continue advocating for the Chinese somehow, of course, but to leave 920…She asked Nathaniel for time to think, and spent the night in prayer and contemplation.

Nathaniel

The next morning, she said yes. Nathaniel beamed, and Mary and Gertrude, when they heard the news, rushed ecstatically into her arms. Donaldina felt peaceful happiness welling up within her. It seemed as if our heroine was finally coming to the end of her career at 920 Sacramento Street, and would have the pleasure of her own home.

The train clickity-clacked back across the thousands of miles of America. Its whistle sounded like a veritable song of laughter, and the colors of the autumn palette glowed with spectacular radiance. At the age of forty-one, Donaldina Cameron would be a bride. Her sister Annie met her at the train station, brought her home for a slice of lemon meringue pie, and was the first to hear the news.

Donaldina believed that the mission home would be able to continue without her. Nora Bankes would make a fine superintendent, and Tien Wu, recently returned from six years of education in the East, would be a stellar help. Donaldina told only two people at 920 of her approaching wedding, holding back news that she knew would be greeted with lamentation. Her friends and daughters would be happy for her, but would dread her departure, and she did not wish to create a spectacle. Working the next several months as intensely as ever, Donaldina prepared herself for the transition from one stage of life to the next.

Nathaniel came to visit. He admired Donaldina's poised calm in the midst of chaos, calling her "the eye of the storm." She gratefully replied that he must be seeing the fruit of her attempt to remember the presence of God throughout the day. Autumn gave way to winter and so very soon winter melted to spring. Donaldina hid her deep emotion as she presided over her last annual meeting.

She and Nathaniel planned their wedding for July 26, her birthday, in Japan, with a honeymoon in China. Her wardrobe was ready, neatly set aside for departure. She tried to mentally untangle herself from 920 and prepare for her new life ahead.

Early in July, Donaldina received a telegram. She opened it and read:

Lean hard and take courage. Stop. Father died today. Stop. Mary Tooker.

Donaldina staggered to her room, stunned. Later she learned that Nathaniel had collapsed suddenly while on an errand downtown. Donaldina wept, she grieved, she mourned, but in private. Few could sympathize with her, for few had known of her new happiness. It helped to write to Mary and Gertrude, but not many at the home understood why Lo Mo's eyes were often red and swollen, or why her appetite had disappeared.

In August, Donaldina requested a six-month leave, which the concerned board immediately granted. She travelled to Southern California to visit her sisters and Allan, but she was still available to the home and was often called for the most troublesome problems. Recovery did not come. To really rest, she needed more distance from San Francisco. So it was decided that Donaldina would accompany her niece Caroline on a trip to Hawaii.

Caroline was thrilled at the prospect of uninterrupted time with Aunt Dolly, and the exhausted Donaldina's sense of adventure started to revive as they boarded their ship. They discovered that their small cabin was filled with flowers and gifts, loving well wishes from friends. The anchor was lifted, the ship moved towards open sea, and they went back to settle into their room where–surprise!–a Chinese girl peered out at Caroline from behind a cabinet. Donaldina smiled and quickly explained to her shocked niece that this just-rescued girl would be traveling with them to Hawaii; from there, she would be able to safely return to her home in China. Even on this ship, Aunt Dolly could not fully escape her work.

Under the Hawaiian sun, Donaldina was released from the exhausting entanglements of her demanding responsibilities. She was

Nathaniel

able to think in quiet privacy about Nathaniel Tooker and how he had blessed her life. She was restored in body and spirit. A few weeks later, as she once more passed through the Golden Gate to her "great, grey city," she yearned to be home with her girls at 920.

Donaldina and one of her little girls

Chapter Thirteen
Love Never Dies

博愛

Do not hand over the life of your dove to wild beasts;
Do not forget the lives of your afflicted people forever.
Have regard for your covenant,
Because haunts of violence fill the dark places of the land.
Psalm 74:19-20

Ah King and Ah Young toiled each day and were rarely allowed outside. Not once but twice had they bravely sent pleas to 920, and not once but twice had Donaldina attempted a rescue. Yet both rescue missions failed; the wily owner was ever aware of Donaldina and, to her consternation, outwitted her on both occasions.

Until one September evening, that is. Donaldina, humming as she came down the stairs, was stopped short by the sight of Tien Wu's distressed face.

"Lo Mo! Ah King and Ah Young have been seen! They're coming this way now, on Jackson Street. They're soon to be transported to Oakland."

Instantly, Donaldina shifted into rescue mode. There was not a spare second to go searching for a reliable police officer, so Donaldina,

Tien Wu, and their visiting friend Reverend Ecclestone bolted out the door and into the darkening dusk.

"Hst! Over here!" whispered Donaldina, and the group ducked into the entryway of an herbal shop. Neat bundles of drying herbs were piled on countertops and hung from the roof inside; layers of pungent smells penetrated the air. Donaldina whispered to her comrades. "Wait for my word. When the time comes, Reverend Ecclestone, you will accost the adults. I'm not sure how many there will be, but we're taking them by surprise; I'm sure you can manage them." The Reverend chuckled wryly at her confidence in his ability as Donaldina continued. "Meanwhile, Tien Wu and I will run with the girls."

They waited silently inside the doorway for three or four minutes, then Donaldina's body tensed, and she said in a low voice, "That'll be them." They bolted out and into the path of the unsuspecting party of three–fortunately, Ah King and Ah Young had only one escort. The interpreter motioned, "Here! Quickly! Girls, it's Lo Mo from the mission home. We're here to help you. Run with us!" Reverend Ecclestone fulfilled his pastoral duty by shoving the guard to the side, while Ah King and Ah Young, with hardly any hesitation, dashed to the end of the block with Lo Mo and the interpreter.

"Taxi!" bellowed Donaldina, and with impeccable timing, a driver pulled up. Two girls and their three rescuers piled in on top of each other. "Now!" hollered Donaldina. "We must leave now! Quick, man! Quick!" Two other tong men had joined the girls' escort, anger etched on their faces, and they were running but a few feet away from the taxi. "Go straight, no time to turn around, we'll circle back to Sacramento Street." The discombobulated driver tried to decipher the gasping directions while Lo Mo, as she spoke, reached out and placed her hands gently over those of the two trembling girls.

Several weeks later, Donaldina recounted this story to her brother Allan and his family at the San Benito Valley ranch. They sat again around the big farm table as the late afternoon sun streamed through the window. A visit from Aunt Dolly was always a treat. She never failed to bring thrilling stories as well as some good laughs. And Allan's ranch was Donaldina's precious refuge from the stress and strain of Sacramento Street. She let her eyes linger on the oak tree, reveling in how the breeze moved through the leaves, twirling them cheerfully.

Donaldina (in the rear) and her siblings, with brother Allan in front. Courtesy of Donaldina Klingen.

This particular visit was one she would always remember with bittersweet ache. After Donaldina returned to San Francisco, Allan, who had been healthy all his life, was suddenly struck with a mysterious and vicious ailment. She rushed back to be with him. Three days later, her only brother died. Dolly felt once more like the bereaved little girl whose mother could not come with her to pick wildflowers. She and her sister Annie stood together under the big oak, holding hands and watching the sun slowly sink below the horizon.

"Love never dies, Dolly," Annie reminded her younger sister gently. Within grief burned hope. She would see Allan again. In the meantime, she would go back to San Francisco determined to show every person under her care that love never dies.

A whirlwind of international events shook millions worldwide and brought changes to life at 920. Conflict that had been ravaging Europe for years now came to America: On April 6, 1917, the United States officially joined the Great War.

Donaldina and her household were eager to contribute what they could. The home became a branch of the Junior Red Cross. Former slaves knit socks and scarves with patriotic fervor, even though immigration law prohibited them from becoming U.S. citizens. Donaldina noticed that since so many men were fighting overseas, farms around San Francisco were suffering from neglect. She proposed that her young women help harvest crops. Farmers were extraordinarily skeptical that Chinese orphan girls and former prostitutes could adequately complete the work, but Donaldina, ever-persuasive, was able at last to convince the owner of an apricot orchard to hire them. Those who were selected for this venture took great enjoyment in the thrill of camping out in the orchard with twenty of their sisters. They also satisfied the farmer and earned some income. Word spread to neighboring farms, and summer fruit harvesting became a mission house tradition.

The War to End All Wars ended in 1918. Next came the devastating influenza epidemic. The flu pervaded 920 with ferocious savagery. They created makeshift infirmaries where they anxiously nursed fevers night and day. After weeks of suspense, every resident emerged a survivor. Finally, after war and flu, the home resumed its routines of studying and sewing, housekeeping and hospitality, visits to the court and Angel Island, and occasional special events or jaunts out of Chinatown.

A milestone approached. April of 1920 would be the twenty-fifth anniversary of Donaldina's work at 920 Sacramento Street. Tien

Wu, eager to celebrate this event, wrote to alumni of the home and to many of Donaldina's other friends, inviting them to visit for the occasion. Responses to these letters included an unexpectedly large pile of monetary gifts. As cash continued to heap up on her desk, Tien Wu puzzled over what to do with this love offering. When she approached Donaldina, the latter was resolute. She did not want a single gift. She needed nothing. When told that gifts had already been given, Donaldina told Tien Wu to set up a scholarship in her name at a school for blind children in China. But Tien Wu and the girls were dissatisfied with this. Many friends had indicated that they especially wanted their gifts to be spent for something personal and special for Lo Mo. So Tien Wu and her co-conspirators secretly plotted to renovate Lo Mo's bedroom, which looked as weary and worn as Chinatown alleys after days of rain.

Conveniently, Donaldina was scheduled to speak at a conference in San Diego shortly before the anniversary party. As soon as Lo Mo left, workmen came to sand the floors and paint the walls, while the girls of the home gleefully planned how they would transform the room into a beautiful masterpiece, filling it with tokens of love and affection.

Meanwhile, in San Diego, Donaldina bumped down a road in a streetcar on her way to meetings. She was enjoying the company of four of her daughters, the quartet of 920 who sang for special events. Ida Lee, an alumna who now lived in southern California, had also joined them.

Life with Donaldina Cameron was never boring. Suddenly, an inexplicable intuition nudged her to get off the bus. Rather than abandon this hunch for a more rational approach to life, Donaldina turned to Ida. "I have to go. Please take care of the girls. I'll meet you at the conference." Before the bewildered Ida could reply, Donaldina had stepped off.

Donaldina started walking down the street. Within moments, she was hailed by an astonished acquaintance who ran up to her, shouting, "Miss Cameron! How is this possible? I was about to phone you in San Francisco! And you are right here! It is a disaster. I need your help."

The story stumbled out in fragments. A girl was in trouble. Her name was Suey Seen, a slave who had recently been rescued by a man who loved her. Her former owner aggressively pursued them. Desperate, the couple planned to escape to China. To procure money for tickets, the man robbed a store. He had a gun. The storeowner had a gun. The storeowner was killed. The lover was in jail. Suey Seen was wounded, in the hospital, and facing charges of robbery and murder. Donaldina interrupted her friend, "Where's the hospital? We'll go there now. Keep talking."

Suey Seen was hysterical. She writhed in her hospital bed, terrified, as withdrawal from opium addiction exacerbated the pain from her bullet wound. Two nurses had to restrain her from committing suicide. Donaldina came and confidently took charge of the situation. She phoned the still slightly flummoxed Ida Lee and requested that she come to the hospital to translate. She arranged for someone else to take her place at the meetings. She telegraphed 920 to inform them that her return would be delayed.

Back at 920, Tien Wu and the girls were dismayed, though not surprised, to hear that a rescue mission would postpone Lo Mo. Here they were, ecstatic about the approaching gala, while the celebrant was out gallivanting in the streets of San Diego saving people. Oh, how they hoped that she would make it back in time for her party! But the delay did allow more time for Donaldina's bedroom transformation. The worn, rough floor now gleamed with stylish hardwood, enhanced by an exquisite blue Chinese rug. Cracks in the trimming and walls were sealed, and on top of the fresh coat of white paint hung delicately-flowered wallpaper. Fresh sheets, new curtains, and a homespun bedspread completed the room. An enticing haven of calm was created in the middle of the bustling home.

Love Never Dies

In San Diego, Donaldina spent half of her waking hours sitting on courtroom benches, waiting to talk to the authorities who could give permission for Suey Seen to travel to San Francisco, where she could recover before her trial, in a safe place away from henchmen. She spent the other half of her waking hours sitting in a hospital chair, trying to gain the trust of the battered, frightened woman. Suey Seen was suspicious of this white-haired foreigner, but she gradually, tentatively, began to place a bit of confidence in the woman who kept visiting and who spoke so kindly. Once Suey Seen trusted Donaldina, they could more easily secure permission from the court and the doctors to move her to San Francisco.

After several days, they were ready to go home. Suey Seen's wounds still required attention, and she still convulsed from opium withdrawal, but Donaldina convinced the doctors of her nursing capability, and Ida Lee would travel with them to translate and help. They booked a bedroom car on the train. Suey Seen cried out often in physical pain and mental torment; Donaldina and Ida stayed by her side.

Donaldina arrived at 920 with nary a moment to spare. It was the morning of the twenty-fifth anniversary party and the house was a flurry of excitement. Some guests had already arrived. Shouts of joy greeted Lo Mo, and girls flocked to the door, not in the least surprised to see their beloved mother emerge from the taxi half carrying a thin, sickly looking girl. Tien Wu met her on the stairs. "Quick, Tien," instructed Donaldina, "She's very sick. Her wound is starting to hemorrhage. Hurry. Call the doctor."

The household, accustomed to crisis, quickly adjusted so that party preparations could continue while the doctor was called and a bed was made up for the patient. Food was prepared for her and people were enlisted to sit with her. After the doctor's visit, Donaldina started to explain Suey Seen's story to Tien Wu. Before she was quite finished, however, Tien Wu interrupted, "Miss Cameron," she remonstrated, "your shoulders are shaking. You are completely spent. I will take care of everything. Go upstairs to your room and rest."

The time for the unveiling of the bedroom renovation had arrived. Would Lo Mo be angry that they had disregarded her request for the gifts to be sent to the school in China? Tien Wu couldn't be sure. They walked together up the stairs and to the threshold, where Tien Wu stayed at the open door just long enough to hear Donaldina draw in her breath. Then Tien Wu slipped away–perhaps to let Lo Mo enjoy her gift in privacy, or perhaps to let any possible anger at their disobedience cool.

Donaldina's beautiful room moved her deeply. She recognized love embedded in each detail. After shedding a few tears of exhausted joy, she knelt for a prayer of thanksgiving. Then she noticed more gifts sitting on the newly polished dresser, including a charming lace dress, silver shoes, and a note from her old, faithful friend Eleanor Olney: "Dolly, will you wear this tonight for your girls, who are disappointed that time will not allow the brocade to be made up? Hope the slippers won't pinch your toes."

Donaldina gathered her thoughts in the lovely bedroom sanctuary for a few minutes before changing into her party attire. Then, donned in Eleanor's dress, she gracefully entered the festivities and greeted her guests. Donaldina looked luminous as she mingled with her visitors–friends, alumni, immigration officials, pastors. All the diverse people she had met and worked with during twenty-five years in Chinatown seemed to be represented by the scores who came to call. More gifts were given, several of them elegant and expensive. But the best of all came unexpectedly from the upstairs infirmary.

There had been some awkward discomfort in the house that evening when occasional shrieks and groans penetrated the happy hum of merry-making. Suey Seen was delirious and in pain. The guests did not know the source of the screams, and might misunderstand. Donaldina wanted to go to Suey Seen, but Tien Wu convinced her that her place tonight was with her guests. Later, the disconcerting sounds quieted, and Tien found a moment to pull Donaldina aside and slip an opal ring onto her finger. "From Suey Seen," said Tien Wu in a low voice. "I was able to capture her attention when her mind was clear for a few seconds. I told her that it is a special anniversary day for you and that your friends are giving you a party. She stopped shaking and it seems she really understood. She looked at me straight in the eye, took off her ring, and asked me to give it to you and tell you that she will stay at 920 and learn from the woman called Lo Mo. She wants to promise that she will be a good daughter to you, if you will teach her."

Lo Mo caressed the ring between the thumb and index finger of her other hand; the slight smile her visitors might have seen hinted at her deep joy. She turned back to the party, moving toward a guest who looked in need of attention.

Donaldina relished every moment of the festivities, which lasted late into the night. When she finally closed the doors of 920, she exhaled deeply. As her eyes wandered over the piles of gifts, she heard sudden, angry shouts and gunshots ringing in the streets. Chinatown was tense with another bout of fighting between rival tongs, precipitated by a heart-wrenching story that involved an enslaved young woman who had been brought to the home. Donaldina thought of the many, many friends she had enjoyed today, and remembered that she also had enemies. Lately, some had been saying that Donaldina Cameron was the most loved and the most hated figure in Chinatown. But it was the love that would endure.

Love never dies. It had been a good day. Tomorrow the work would continue.

Chapter Fourteen
Mae and Manion

友愛

*Once in an age God sends to some of us a friend who loves in us,
not a false-imagining, an unreal character, but looking through the rubbish
of our imperfections, loves in us the divine ideal of our nature,
—loves, not the man that we are, but the angel that we may be.*
Harriet Beecher Stowe

Mae's story is tragically similar to the stories of others in this book. She lived in a rural Chinese village. Her mother sold her to a Chinese-American man. This man sold her for his own profit. Mae's innocence was destroyed and she was psychologically and physically ravaged. She hated her life and wished it would end.

Mae's story is tragically different from the stories of others in this book. You see, Mae had a brother. She and her brother, Kim, were very good friends. Years before Mae was sold, Kim had immigrated to America with light in his eyes and hope for his future. But life in San Francisco proved to be hard, and like many other young men in similar situations, Kim soon began to associate with a gang in Chinatown. He joined the Sing Dong Tong and became a hatchetman, hired to do the work of assassinations. He was admired as a man who could get the job done with panache and charisma. He was nefarious for his daring courage. Even his name changed. No one called him Kim anymore. He now went by Louie Sam.

Mae did not know what had become of her brother Kim, but she often thought of him. When she was fourteen years old, she naïvely believed the man who told her that he would give her an education and rich husband in America. Instead, he sold her as a concubine to a middle-aged man named Jue Yat. She was transported to San Francisco from Canton and taken to the apartment where she would live with him and his wife and children. Comparatively speaking, life as a concubine was usually better than life as a prostitute. But Mae was miserable. She dreamed of finding her brother.

Jue Yat happened to be in the same tong as Louie Sam. To celebrate his acquisition of a beautiful new concubine, Jue Yat threw a party. As a part of the tong, Louie Sam was there at the party.

When Louie Sam saw Mae, something deep within him stirred. Was he attracted to her sweet face and dainty body? Naturally. Yet there was something else. A spark of recognition. A whisper from his past. Louie Sam left the party that night bewildered and disturbed, determined to discover who this concubine was. Jue Yat, meanwhile, noticed the way that Louie Sam gazed intensely at his property, and determined to keep a close watch on him.

Soon, Kim realized that Mae was his sister, and his brotherly love for her awakened. With much skill and finagling, Kim arranged to speak to Mae, revealed himself as her brother, and promised that she would not remain in bondage for long. He would rescue her and bring her to the House on the Hill.

Snatching the concubine of a fellow tong member and taking her to the despised Donaldina Cameron was unthinkable. And so Louie Sam tried a different approach. He took a pen in hand and wrote a note to be delivered to 920 Sacramento: "Miss, you go pretty quick to 243 Jos Alley 36, Jue Yat place to catch one small slave girl. I am a highbinder and cannot come to your house. I don't like my sister to be in such a place. Hurry quick."

To receive notes pleading a rescue was a frequent occurrence at 920, but to receive a note from a hatchetman asking for help was certainly unusual. Donaldina mused silently at the way the perpetrator had, in an odd sense, become the victim.

A warrant was procured to search the address in the note, but to no avail. Jue Yat denied that he possessed a slave girl and smiled placidly when a thorough search of the apartment seemed to justify his assertion. A disgruntled group of rescuers returned to 920.

Jue Yat, suspicious that a raid was soon to come, had secreted Mae away to a nearby brothel for safekeeping. A customer named Lum Ming who frequented that brothel took a liking to Mae.

"Mae," he cajoled, "Mae, listen to me. I want to be your friend." She recoiled from Lum Ming, but day after day, he approached her with the same message, until she began to believe that maybe there was such a thing as a trustworthy man in this world after all. "Mae. You hate it here, don't you?" he said one day, "I can see nothing but distaste in your stony face. I will help you run away. I will take you to the House on the Hill." The House on the Hill. That was where Kim had promised to take her. And so Mae, who had not yet lost hope in humanity, agreed to the plan.

But Lum Ming never intended to take Mae to the House on the Hill. Instead he took her to his apartment and locked her up.

Three men now vied for Mae. Jue Yat, furious about the kidnapping, wanted his expensive concubine back. Lum Ming was determined to hold onto the girl he had so cleverly stolen. And Louie Sam was secretly livid that both men had dared put hands on his sister.

A meeting of the Sing Dong Tong was called with the intent of determining the appropriate course of action for recovering Jue Yat's stolen property. The men gathered in a small upper room thick with the sticky scent of incense. In silence, they assembled around an enormous, ornately carved table.

Fierce Compassion

When everyone was seated, the Master of the Tong called the meeting to order: "Let the first oath be recited." A liturgy of solemn oaths followed. The men swore fidelity to the tong and threatened death to any who attempted treachery.

After these opening ceremonies, the tong decided to demand that the offender, Lum Ming, return Jue Yat's concubine. If immediate compliance ensued, no harm would come to Lum Ming or his tong.

Lum Ming refused to return Mae, but offered a grand sum of six thousand dollars to keep her in his possession. Jue Yat spurned this offer. Lum Ming would not budge. And so the Sing Dong Tong ruled that Lum Ming must die. The assassin was about to be chosen by lot when Louie Sam stood and said, "I will do the task."

Jue Yat was instantly wary. He remembered how Louie Sam had stared at Mae the night of the party. But few were surprised at this offer. Louie Sam was brave, young, and always thirsting for adventure. Since no ulterior motive was known, the tong granted Louie Sam the task of killing Lum Ming and returning Mae.

Now we introduce yet another character in the thickening plot. Lum Bing was an old, derelict man who was so deeply addicted to opium that his life hung on being able to buy enough of the drug each day. Lum Bing's opium supplier was his distant kinsman, Lum Ming.

Louie Sam and his assistant marched into Lum Bing's miniscule, destitute apartment. The assistant pinned the old man down while Louie Sam held a knife to his throat, "Tell us what we want to know and you will live. If you lie or refuse, I will slit your throat."

Lum Bing's eyes rolled about in their sockets, "You would kill an innocent old man?"

"At what time of day do you go to your kinsman, Lum Ming, to purchase your opium?" Lum Bing answered, and they asked another question, and another, until they were satisfied that they had all the details vital to the success of their mission. When that task had been completed, part two of the elaborate plan was enacted. The assistant stayed with Lum Bing, keeping him at gunpoint, while Louie Sam went and fetched Fong Gim.

Fong Gim was known as the best make-up artist in all of California. For a tidy sum of one hundred dollars, Fong Gim agreed to go with Louie Sam back to Lum Bing's apartment. Hours passed. From the outside, the little apartment in the alley showed no signs of life. Finally, a man pushed open the door and hobbled out. Anyone living in the alley would have easily identified him as Lum Bing, with his stooped walk, his stringy, white beard, his deeply wrinkled face and the smell of opium clinging like fleas to his withered skin. It was time for his daily outing to procure his drug. Even the police that patrolled those streets recognized him and called out a greeting.

As usual, Lum Bing halted at the doorstep of his kinsman, Lum Ming. He knocked on the door, the secret knock, five light taps of five fingers on one hand, then a pause, then five light taps of five fingers on the other hand. The door opened enough for Lum Bing to enter, and was immediately shut behind him.

The instant the latch on the door clicked, Lum Bing was Lum Bing no more. He was the hatchetman Louie Sam, the infuriated brother Kim. Not two seconds later, a bullet exploded through Lum Ming's temple and he was left to die in his own blood. A woman watched in horror.

"Take me to the girl," commanded Louie Sam.

"I don't know what you're talking about." A gun pointed at her chest persuaded her otherwise, and Louie Sam was led to a back room.

"Mae! It's me, Kim." She recognized his voice even through the disguise. Kim gently guided his sister to the door. Brother and sister fled from the building and into the waiting taxicab. Who can say what transpired between the two during that short drive to 920 Sacramento Street? They soon arrived at their destination. Kim helped Mae up the steps, knocked on the door, and left.

Fierce Compassion

Like so many others, Mae thrived under the loving care of Lo Mo and the sympathy of new friends who understood her sufferings, but her happiness was tainted. Upon arriving at 920, she immediately asked about the safety of her brother. Donaldina sighed. When she heard the story of what had happened, she knew there would be a very high price for the head of Louie Sam–from two tongs. He had killed a member of one, and betrayed the other by bringing a concubine to the mission house.

News of Kim's death came within twenty-four hours. He made his escape from San Francisco, but as soon as he stepped off of the train in Fresno, he was shot dead.

The story of these murders made headlines. San Francisco's newspaper readers speculated about the possible connections between the two murders, but few knew the true story. Police in cities across the United States were alerted to keep a close watch on the Chinese population. This had the potential of igniting a new tong war.

"Greater love hath no one than this," Donaldina whispered, half to herself, half to the girl who sobbed beside her, "that a man lay down his life for his friends."

The fears and austerity of World War I melted away into innovation, creativity, and change. Jazz and dance clubs, radio, moving pictures, and mass-produced automobiles burst forth. The United States optimistically aspired to world economic dominance. Meanwhile, on the other side of the Pacific, centuries of Manchurian dynastic rule had crumbled, and the fight for the future of China was underway, as Sun Yat Sen, Chiang Kai Shek, and Mao Zedong each gathered supporters. But amidst the swirling excitement and change of the 1920s, Chinatown seemed stuck in the past.

A new wave of tong violence, precipitated by the murders of Lum Ming and Louie Sam, ruptured throughout California. Bodies

Mae and Manion

piled up as each side tried to stay ahead in the death tally. Chinatown reverberated with gunshot, fearful citizens stayed off the streets, and business came to a standstill as merchants were forced into hiding.

After nine months, the local government decided it was time to interfere. Police Chief Daniel O'Brien appointed his friend Sergeant Jack Manion as chief of the Chinatown police squad. His orders were simple: take sixteen men with you to Chinatown and make the fighting stop.

Rumor among the tongs was that Jack Manion was poor and that he had children to feed. Bribing him should henceforth be easy. Gang leaders would pay their respects, feel him out, and then get him on their side and out of their business.

Someone else was equally intent on meeting the new police chief. When Jack Manion arrived for his appointment at 920 Sacramento Street, Donaldina welcomed him warmly. "Sergeant Manion," she began as she led her visitor to her office, "I cannot tell you how thankful I have been for the support of the Chinatown police squad. It has been an invaluable source of assistance to us over the course of our work and I look forward to the help which you and your men will undoubtedly give to us, and we to you." This invitation to partnership was greeted with a stiff nod and bow from the Sergeant, followed by a rather cool silence. *Well,* ruminated Donaldina, *this doesn't look promising. Those wretched criminals have probably already parleyed with him and hinted to him of their jewels and gold coins. I wonder how much it took to get him on their side. Oh well, I shan't give up until I know for sure.*

A girl came and dropped off a tray with two steaming cups. "Tea?" Without waiting for a reply, Donaldina placed a cup in the officer's hands. "Sergeant Manion, I am entirely willing to assist you in your work. I've twenty-five years of experience here. I can navigate you through Chinatown's alleys and Chinatown's opium dens and Chinatown's every vile brothel. I understand the challenges that the hard-working, law-abiding Chinese face, and I can tell you who your friends are. The last sergeant relied on my advice and I in turn relied on his support. When we cooperate, we make an effective team."

Manion maintained his succinct tone. "Thank you, Miss Cameron." There they sat, sipping tea. The new police chief responded to her congenial advances with few words, even when she tried to warm him up by inquiring about his family. *Oh, bother those crooked politicians and corrupted police and nefarious tongs*, thought Donaldina.

Sergeant Manion rose to depart. Suddenly, the pealing bells of Old St. Mary's Catholic Church resonated throughout 920. Donaldina had heard that Jack Manion was a devout Catholic, and she was struck with sudden inspiration. She moved towards Manion, touched his sleeve, and pointed him towards the west window, looking out over Chinatown at the church. The sound of the bells faded as the last red-gold rays of sunset enveloped the steeple of St. Mary's, setting its cross afire. "Sergeant Manion, I want you to see this sight!" She pointed to the cross, waited until his eyes fixed on it, and then spoke, quietly and firmly, "That cross is the symbol of the One we both love and serve." She watched Jack Manion's stiff features slowly soften into a reflective smile, "It is that," he said softly, "It is that, Miss Cameron." Then he looked down at her with a broader smile and continued, "And we might be doing a better job of serving Him if we tackled Chinatown together."

From that day on, the Irish police officer and Scottish mission matron worked together as an incorrigible pair. Donaldina's fears of tong influence over Jack Manion proved to be happily unnecessary. Sergeant Manion was determined to eradicate Chinatown of its crime. The tong leaders sat down to pay their token respects to the new police boss, following their polite formalities with hints of bribes. Manion replied bluntly to all advances of obsequious circumvention: "It's all off. There's a new deal. No more killings. No more opium. No more slave girls. Businessmen must be safe. Step out of line and you will be arrested and deported." They nodded and smiled, pretended compliance, and even signed a document accepting their

Mae and Manion

responsibility to end the crime in Chinatown, with every intent that their kingdoms would continue as usual. But then Sergeant Manion picked up the document on which they had signed their names and conspicuously placed it into his pocket with a sincere promise that the next time there was a murder in Chinatown, this evidence would allow him to order them all deported. The complacent gang leaders suddenly felt the ground tremble beneath them.

When news of this encounter reached Donaldina's ears, she laughed out loud. For the next several months, she watched with utmost pleasure as Manion's squad of young Irishmen went hard after narcotics, gambling, and brothels.

Sergeant Manion and Miss Cameron met often, while Jack's daughter Agnes played under the big table. Jack Manion's energy renewed Donaldina Cameron's hope that they might finally be able to abolish Chinese slavery in the United States. His officers were under strict orders to give Miss Cameron anything she asked for. Sometimes they balked at this. Donaldina was accustomed to making life and death decisions quickly, sometimes faster than the pace of proper procedure allowed. But Manion insisted that his men follow her intuition, and soon Donaldina "counted on Providence and Jack Manion to help her disarm the tongs."

The Chinese law-breakers enjoyed pitting their wits against this new adversary, and they grudgingly grew in their respect for Sergeant Manion. Meanwhile, the rest of Chinatown started to appreciate the new safety of the streets. Jack Manion, like Donaldina Cameron, became both a beloved and a hated figure in Chinatown. As years passed, Chinatown's appreciation manifested itself in a touching tribute. Those twelve blocks of San Francisco started to welcome a generation of baby girls and boys named Jack, Manion, Donald, Donaldina, and Cameron.

Sergeant Jack Manion with a girl from Chinatown.

Chapter Fifteen
Allies Near and Far

友情

For he will deliver the needy who cry out,
the afflicted who have no one to help.
He will take pity on the weak and the needy
and save the needy from death.
He will rescue them from oppression and violence,
for precious is their blood in his sight.
Psalm 72:12-14

"Good afternoon," said the young man, as Donaldina extended her hand to him, "My name is Charles Shepherd. You must be the famed Donaldina Cameron."

"It's a pleasure to meet you."

The others in the room momentarily faded away as the two sized each other up. Charles noticed Miss Cameron's elegant dress and the abundant white hair under her stylish hat. He thought that her eyes were unquestionably sympathetic, but also shone with a gleam of quiet defiance. Donaldina meanwhile observed a handsome young man who seemed ardent but slightly uncomfortable in this room, which was buzzing with conversation among Chinatown's Christian leaders and social activists.

Donaldina broke the silence, "What brings you to Chinatown, Mr. Shepherd?"

"Well, I've just come from Shanghai to take up my post as the Director of Baptist Chinese Missions in the United States. But honestly, I'm not sure how I will make a useful contribution. It seems there is plenty of work going on here already. Look at this room, full of people."

"I would certainly like to talk with you more," said Donaldina, pulling a card out of her bag, "but I believe our meeting is about to commence. Would you care to join me for tea at four tomorrow afternoon? The Presbyterian Mission Home is just up the hill from the Baptist Church, and looks quite similar. We're the other big brick building studded with those charming clinker bricks, souvenirs from our earthquake."

The meeting began, but Donaldina only half-listened. Instead, she was busy planning Charles Shepherd's future. Several years ago, with much support from the Tooker sisters, she had finally opened an extension to 920 across the bay in Oakland, for the littlest girls. The teens and other women that came to them were often rough and roguish in language and behavior as they recovered from abuse and drug addiction. Donaldina sometimes cringed at their influence over the young ones. She had fervently desired to open a new home so that the smallest children could have their own happy, protected space. They had it now, and dozens of girls found shelter in the house named after the Tookers. But there was another need that had been bothering her.

The following day, Charles arrived precisely on time. Donaldina welcomed him with a smile.

After they chatted a bit, Donaldina led her guest to her chosen topic of conversation. "Mr. Shepherd," she said, leaning forward in her chair, "I rather think that you are searching for your calling here."

"Indeed, I have come from Shanghai to San Francisco and have found only restlessness. I see that there are many needs, but don't know where I fit."

Allies Near and Far

"I have a proposal that could occupy you for a good while. Right now, staying here at our home for girls, there are five young boys. They, like you, are trying to find their place. Boys are always showing up at the door: orphaned, or abandoned, or brought by impoverished parents who want us to care for and educate their sons. We can't lodge them here for long–this institution is designed for girls. And yet I am loath to turn them away."

Charles' face conveyed surprise. "In China, sons are valued by their families far more than girls. I can hardly believe that they might be abandoned here."

"This is not China, and things are very different. Mr. Shepherd, we and our Methodist friends have for years devoted ourselves to caring for needy girls; but no one has ever seemed to think about the boys. I tell you people bring them here constantly, and it grieves us to turn them away to who knows what misery and degradation. There is a man in Chinatown like Oliver Twist's Fagin. He picks up boys and trains them to steal. The boys need protection from those who would take advantage of them. They need education for their minds and beauty for their imaginations. They need to be told the stories of valiant heroes, trained in the habits of a Christian home, and shown that they can have purpose in life.

"Now, making a home for these boys would be no easy task. You would have to convince people of the need, raise funds, secure a location. It would be hard to find a suitable space in these cramped blocks of Chinatown, and once you go outside, not everyone is eager to have Chinese neighbors. But it would be very worthwhile, and I believe you could do it."

Charles Shepherd left the house on the hill that afternoon with a new spring in his step. Soon after, he enthusiastically started to work on creating a home for Chinese boys. In the meantime, he also became an ally to Donaldina on rescues. He enjoyed wearing disguises, slipping in and out of streets and shops dressed as a ragged, cap-topped wanderer.

Fierce Compassion

Four years later, the Chung Mei home for boys opened on Ninth Street in Berkeley. Three hundred people came to celebrate its dedication day. Donaldina entrusted Charles with seven boys who had been living at 920. George Chow, Adam Wu, Walter Lim, Frank Louie, George Haw, Howard Deah, and Benjie Wu now had their own home–and best of all, it was not swarming with girls! Charles Shepherd became affectionately known as "Captain," and, eventually, eight hundred boys grew under his care at Chung Mei.

After thirty years of labor, Donaldina Cameron now found herself as a prominent leader of the now-popular cause to end Chinese slavery. While Charles Shepherd, Jack Manion, and the mission house staff continued the front line battles at home in San Francisco, Donaldina traveled across the country with Tien Wu. They advocated for more just immigration laws and visited supporters and former residents of the home. Wherever they went, they were guaranteed a warm welcome and a roof over their heads, for Donaldina's daughters had spread out across America.

They rode east on the rails built by Chinese men fifty years earlier. In Detroit, a daughter of one of Donaldina's daughters listened, with rapt attention, to the stories of 920, and then emptied her piggy bank to give to the home in San Francisco. In Philadelphia, puzzled streetcar passengers watched an elegant-looking lady step off to excited greetings from the Chinese children running toward her. Lo Mo had acquired another new name: many chubby-faced Chinese toddlers called her "Lo Pau," Grandma. As hearth fires crackled, Donaldina spun riveting bedtime stories to children about the adventures she had shared with their mamas.

Donaldina was scheduled to meet with men from the Department of Labor in Washington, D.C. to whom she could explain the Chinese slave trade and lobby for laws that would help abolish it. Her friend Dr. Halsey, an old Princeton classmate of Woodrow Wilson, had also arranged a meeting between Donaldina and the president. Donaldina skipped breakfast that morning, preoccupied with planning exactly what she would say to President Wilson. She packed her bag in preparation for the train trip from New York to Washington.

Various connections of Donaldina made it their personal business to know her exact whereabouts in case she was needed. Just before she and Tien Wu left for Washington, D.C., a plea for help came to her hotel room. A girl had been smuggled to Chicago and was on the brink of being sold. Her father in China was desperate.

Donaldina could not get in touch with anyone in Chicago who would be able to help this woman. She looked at the slip of paper in her hand, weighing the needs of the person on the other end of it against her appointment to meet the president of the United States. She hesitated, and then decided to answer the call for help. She found Tien Wu and they bustled outside, called a taxi, embarked on a train for Chicago, and missed the meeting with the president.

Donaldina had managed to arrange for a driver to pick them up in Chicago. This chauffeur had not been told the errand of his passengers, and was rather surprised at the address they gave him, which was not in the part of town he would have expected from these nicely dressed ladies. But once they explained their mission, he entered gallantly into his role as assistant to a rescue. They left Tien Wu in the car, and Donaldina led her new ally up the stairway of an apartment building. Noting that one door was firmly bolted with a solid new lock, she moved in that direction—valuable slaves were always secured. When a man appeared in the hall and glared suspiciously at them, Donaldina took the driver's arm demurely and played the role of a naïve but charming woman who had never seen a Chinese family before. She persuaded him to open the door of the locked apartment. Demureness cast aside, she then surged in and found the victim in a side room. The startled Chinese man disappeared, and they dashed back triumphantly to Tien Wu.

Fierce Compassion

That afternoon, Donaldina met a friend for tea at Marshall Field's. As they sat amid placidly chatting shoppers, she recounted her latest adventure and discovered that this very friend was taking the evening train westbound out of Chicago. Perfect! Donaldina had to go east to Philadelphia, and she had been wondering how she would arrange for the vulnerable young woman to travel safely to San Francisco. She appealed to her friend for help. It was risky to accept responsibility for a recently rescued tong slave, but by the time tea was finished, plans had been made. That evening the escaped slave slipped safely past the tong men who were looking for her at the train station (the driver was called back into action for this feat), and was tucked away in a curtained train bedroom. The household at 920 was alerted to watch for their arrival with a carefully worded telegram, signed with Lo Mo's favorite code name: "Donald Mackenzie."

A telegram sent from Chicago by Donaldina, signed "Donald Mackenzie". Courtesy of Department of Special Collections and University Archives, Stanford University Libraries

Allies Near and Far

Donaldina had an enemy named Oie Kum. Through her beauty and business skill, this slave, also known as Ah Peen or Opium Amy, had become one of the most glamorously adorned and highly sought after prostitutes of Chinatown. After years as a slave, she made enough money, through opium dealing, to pay off her slavery contract and purchase her freedom. Then she started accruing wealth by buying and selling girls herself.

Opium Amy's lucrative business operated just down the hill from the mission home. For years, she and Donaldina Cameron had been pitted against each other in a battle of will and wit. Donaldina's daughters told horrific tales about this woman, so that "the name of Ah-Peen Oie, spoken with shudders by the rescued slave girls who knew her power, was the one name in Chinatown that almost struck terror in the calm heart of Lo Mo."

Ah Peen and Lo Mo met one day under the most unexpected circumstances. A typewritten note arrived at the home asking for help. Donaldina recognized the address: Ah Peen's brothel. Her hand instantly reached for the telephone. "Hello? Yes, Charles. I need you. We've got a call from Ah Peen's place. I'll meet you at the church in seven minutes." She found her interpreter and the two hastened down the steep hill to the Baptist Church, where Charles Shepherd waited.

They quickly moved toward the dark and dreary building, strewn with tattered red Chinese decorations, the smell of cigar smoke hanging in the air. Inside sat Opium Amy, alone. Donaldina gathered her courage. "Stay where you are," she commanded, "We have a note from a girl who needs help and we will not allow you to hinder us." Strangely, Ah Peen did not move, but just watched intently while they searched. They found no one pleading for help, no one hidden away in a secret space. But if Opium Amy had been warned of the rescue and removed her slave, then why would she herself still be sitting here? A sickening thought struck Donaldina. She turned to face her nemesis, and asked quietly, "Ah Peen was it you who sent the note?"

The beautiful, proud woman nodded. She spoke through the interpreter, "My business partner cheated me. I cannot pay my debt. I will be sold again soon, maybe tonight. I will die if this happens. So I ask you, save me."

Donaldina was incredulous and more than a little suspicious. This seemed exactly like a trick that Ah Peen would play to gain power over the girls at 920. Donaldina would not be duped. She turned away and nearly left. But Ah Peen clung to the hem of her dress and began desperately weeping.

"Listen," said Donaldina, "I need time to decide. Are you willing to spend the night in jail? You will be safe there while we decide what to do." Ah Peen agreed.

That night, consternation and heated debate filled the office at 920 as the staff discussed whether to take Opium Amy under their roof. Common sense screamed, "No!" Ah Peen was evil, notorious for her cruelty–many at 920 would testify to this without hesitation. Yet now she pleaded for help. Was it possible that she was sincere?

Although not all the staff agreed with her, Donaldina decided to take Ah Peen, reasoning that it was perhaps not the most just response, but seemed to be the most merciful.

"My Savior has given me great mercy and asks me to follow," Donaldina explained to Ah Peen the next morning. "But," she continued strictly, "you will live in a locked room and you will not take part in the regular activities of our home until I am certain that you do not intend to do harm. If you agree to this, then you may stay at 920."

Ah Peen meekly agreed to the conditions and was moved from the jail cell to the former schoolroom, which had a separate entrance off of Joice Street. A strained hush fell on the house after Ah Peen arrived. The door to her room was regarded with apprehensive fear when the girls timidly tiptoed past. Nightmarish memories rose to the surface, and daily, Donaldina had to remind herself and others:

"Love your enemies. Pray for those who persecute you. Do good to those who hate you."

Each day, Tien Wu brought food and drink to Ah Peen. Soon it was clear that their new resident was severely ill. She was hospitalized, hovering between life and death. It seemed that the desire to live had been sucked out of her, but she eventually recovered enough to return to the schoolroom. She did not cause trouble. But her soul was dark and troubled and she was clearly not yet ready to integrate with the rest of the household.

Another Amy came through the door of 920 at this time. Amy Law was a missionary in China, and she needed a rest. A house full of dozens of girls and women recovering from trauma may seem an odd place for a missionary to stay for vacation, but that is what Amy Law chose. The evening of Miss Law's arrival, she and Miss Cameron sat and exchanged stories. Amy spoke of the thrills and travails of China in that time of revolution and civil war. Donaldina spoke of the thrills and travails of the Chinese in America.

They turned on the new electric lights as night descended on San Francisco. Donaldina thought of Opium Amy sitting alone in her room. "Perhaps the most interesting case we are dealing with right now regards a former prostitute who turned into a slave owner," she told the visiting missionary. Amy's eyebrows rose in interest. Donaldina continued, "She's called Opium Amy." She told the story, ending with the reflection that she did not know how much longer Amy would live and, if she did survive, how she would manage to carve out a normal life after so many years as both recipient and giver of such deceit and malice.

"I think I'll go and meet her tomorrow, if that's all right with you," said Amy. And so Opium Amy met Amy Law. For each day of the missionary's two-week visit, she spent several hours in Ah Peen's room. After Miss Law's departure, Donaldina visited Ah Peen and was amazed to see a new, lightened, even joyful, countenance. Donaldina and Tien Wu were not sure they recognized this woman. She claimed faith in the Christian God and expressed a desire to begin her life anew.

Ah Peen was given freedom in increments. She proved her sincerity by the way she cheerfully accomplished the lowliest of jobs. The former glamorous bad girl of Chinatown scrubbed floors and washed pots and pans. A beautiful picture of redemption emerged as she served the girls in the home, some of whom had once cowed before her as slaves.

One morning, Donaldina woke early to a clattering, crying commotion. Down the red-carpeted stairs she hurried to discover the housekeeper and Ah Peen standing by the door. Tears coursed down Ah Peen's face, and she held a swaddled infant in her arms.

Many years earlier, Ah Peen had given birth to a baby who died. Ever since then, even during her darkest years, she had longed to be a mother. As Ah Peen now held this baby in her arms, she told Donaldina that the night before, she had dreamed that an old man brought her a baby and asked her to care for it, but she had been forced to say no. She woke up weeping. And then the cry of the baby in her dream turned into the cry of the baby who had been left on the doorstep of 920. "I can't let this baby live without me. Not after my dream," she sobbed. Donaldina gazed at the baby and at Ah Peen, and with a hint of a smile she declared, "And there came a man sent from God whose name was John." So they called him John, a baby sent from God to Ah Peen.

In Ah Peen's slave days, a rancher had fallen in love with her. He tried to rescue her, but at that time she had not wanted rescue. Years later, he heard that she was ill at 920 and came to visit. For months and years, he showed a quiet and persistent devotion to Ah Peen, and when little John was three years old, Lo Mo consented to their marriage.

One more story concludes the saga of Ah Peen. She owed money to several men in Chinatown, and was determined to pay her debt, so insisted on working as an employee at her husband's ranch, cooking for guests. She sent money to 920 to be delivered to her creditors, bit by bit, until her debt was cleared. When it came time to pay the last one hundred dollars, Tien Wu told her that the man to whom she owned the money was refusing payment, explaining that he had canceled the debt at the New Year. If Ah Peen really wanted to make the final payment, she would have to come and deliver it herself.

So a meeting was arranged at 920 between the former prostitute and the respected businessman. Seeing him would not be easy for Ah Peen, as it would dredge up the shame of her past life. She walked down the stairs with slow dignity, met him in the office, handed him the money. He told her that he had canceled the debt. But Ah Peen was insistent, and finally he accepted her payment. In a topsy-turvy cultural moment, the merchant bowed respectfully to the prostitute, saying, "If this is your religion, I want to know more of it."

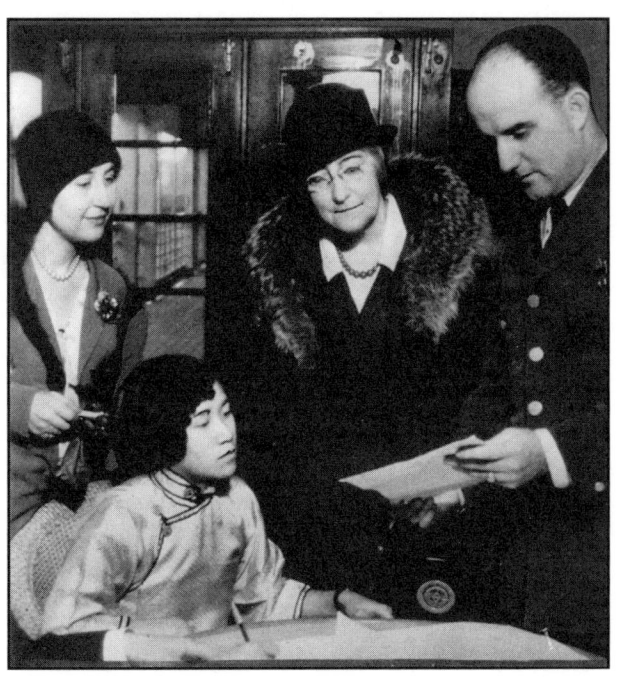

Immigration inspector J.R. McGarth with Donaldina Cameron, Carol Wilson, and Choie Lee, 1931. Used by permission of San Francisco History Center, San Francisco Public Library

Chapter Sixteen
Justice

正義

*Do not turn me over to the desire of my foes,
for false witnesses rise up against me, breathing out violence.*
Psalm 27:12

There is a limit at which forbearance ceases to be a virtue.
John Bunyon

Donaldina sat, knife in hand, at the end of the long table. Mr. Logan sat, knife in hand, at the other end of the long table. In front of each was a sizzling, steaming, savory turkey. It was Thanksgiving, and Donaldina had challenged her visitor to a turkey carving contest. Whoever served half of the guests first would be proclaimed the winner. "Ready? And...Begin!" All enjoyed watching the contestants' skillful carving. Plates were passed quickly down both sides of the table, and "whether a tie resulted because of equal skill or by the gentleman's gallantry, no one was willing to judge."

Laughter from the dining room resounded into the night. Conversation flowed freely among Chinese and American friends. The guests included the genteel Chinese Consul K.L. Kwong, whom Donaldina claimed as a godson, and Lorna Logan, a new addition to the staff, who would become 920's superintendent when Lo Mo retired. This small community enjoyed the refuge of the house on the hill as they took a brief respite from daily burdens made even heavier by the Great Depression.

The next week, Donaldina called a family meeting. "Children," she asked expectantly, "How do you think we could bless our neighbors this Christmas to celebrate God's great gift to us?" Eyes widened, smiles appeared, and a few minutes later, eager chatter accompanied bedtime preparations. Imaginations were stirred and plans discussed.

The Great Depression exacerbated the poverty of Chinatown's residents. The mission home also had to be even more frugal than usual. Pennies were spent with care, and extravagant gifts were not possible, but surely they could do something. So a Christmas celebration was planned for neighbors. What the household lacked in money, they made up for in creativity. Girls carefully wrote invitations. They cooked special treats, rehearsed songs, made and wrapped gifts. They draped tinsel over Chinese lanterns.

On Christmas Day, over fifty children and their mothers came to the door of 920. Faces glowed with exuberance at the promise of a day at the big brick house. The Cameron House hostesses were breathlessly happy after weeks of preparation. Ginger cookies were served next to bowls of steaming rice. After these treats, guests were invited to enjoy a pageant. Behind the door, the 920 girls giggled, scrambling to dress for their parts. Their faces were full of sweetness as they sang tidings of comfort and joy. The story of angels and shepherds, strong Romans, a poor teenage mother, and a baby born to save the world–this was all wondrously new and fresh to many of the participants in the performance as well as to the audience who watched them act out the drama. Then came the thrill of passing out packages to their excited visitors. Taking turns, each resident who had found a home in 920 walked up to a guest to deliver a small, carefully crafted gift. Near the end of the day, one newer daughter hurled herself into

Justice

Lo Mo's arms, exclaiming, "Oh, I like to live in this home! Here I am treated like a daughter of the house; in that other place, I was only a servant!"

The Chinese slave trade in San Francisco and around the country was in decline. One newspaper reported that Donaldina Cameron had rescued over 3,000 girls. Sergeant Manion had recently worked with her on an operation that emptied one of the largest Chinatown brothels. The infamous Opium Amy was now the happy wife of a rancher. More Americans were enlisting to help. The work of 920 was adapting to the changing times. The staff at the house now helped their neighbors find food and work during the Depression and counseled them on how to navigate the challenges of living in two cultures. They advocated for Chinese children in American public schools; they offered marriage counseling and vocational training. However, even though murderous slavery was much less prevalent than it had been, it still lurked. Girls and women were still kidnapped and smuggled into the country to be auctioned and abused.

And still, once in a while, a dramatic story would come to their home; a girl would appear on the step with a horrifying tale. One day, the doorkeeper discovered a young woman whose thin shoulders shook uncontrollably with hysterical sobs, as in a terrified voice she repeated, "Gau mehng a! Gau mehng a!"–Help me!

I have died and I am in hell.

Should I try to run to the mission home? The sailor told me I should, if I ever needed help. But what if he also was lying? "Uncle" promised me a job as a waitress. He lied. Maybe he also lied about the mission home. Or maybe that part was true. Torture by a white devil? I am already tortured every night by white and yellow devils alike. I must escape. I must escape.

Old Wong is bringing me to a parlor to have my hair prepared for tonight. She will not stay to watch me; she will go away until my hair is almost done, then she will return for me. I sit in the chair. She gives instructions and leaves. Does this woman who combs my hair see how my heart nervously flutters? I clear my throat: "Only curl the ends this time." Nearly finished now and Old Wong is not back. The hairdresser is drinking tea in the back room. I might have twenty minutes before they miss me. I grasp the drier above my head, push it away, and walk quickly out to the street, telling myself to look confident.

I try to blend into the crowds. I wish I could run. I wish I could be invisible. I wish I could suddenly cease to exist. There are many people on the streets today, and lots of foreigners shopping on Grant Avenue for Christmas. I want to shout at them and tell them that Grant Avenue is fake. All the pretty things—this is not the real Chinatown. There are dark holes they do not see. I am startled when I think that I recognize faces of men who have jeered at me. Everyone I pass seems to be coming after me. Five times, I slide into a shop and hide myself in rows of satin dresses and porcelain.

It is getting dark and the swaying lanterns point accusing beams of light at me. A salesman taking a jade pin from a display window seems to reach out for me. I do not know where I am going. I grab the arm of a small boy and take him aside, into a space between shops. "Please. Where is the mission home?" He says to turn back in the direction of Sacramento Street, and go up the hill until I pass Stockton and see the big red house on the right. I am sure someone must be chasing me. I must not think about what will happen when I am caught. I feel desperate, like the flies that careen back and forth in the window frame.

Justice

There is the mission home. A few steps. I face a door. Whether they will help me or hurt me I do not know. With shaking hands, I knock.

Kwai Ying's story tumbled out in a torrent of tears. Lo Mo recognized some of the names of her abusers. It seemed that Kwai Ying had been taken by a ring of long-standing slave traders. Many 920 girls had passed through the hands of these same perpetrators, and yet there had never been adequate evidence to take them to court. After hearing Kwai Ying's story, new hope dawned in Donaldina. Kwai Ying remembered many specific details. Perhaps there would now be adequate evidence to prosecute slave traders who had eluded them for years.

Donaldina acted with all due haste. She rang up the assistant United States attorney in San Francisco, who listened intently to the particulars of Kwai Ying's story. When Donaldina stopped talking there was a thoughtful silence before he spoke, "Listen, Miss Cameron. This girl's testimony," another pause ensued before he continued. "I'm fairly certain that she is identifying a large ring of traders. You've heard of the hardware merchant Wong She Duck?"

Donaldina grimly assented. "All who work around Chinatown have heard of Wong She Duck. On the outside he is a respected businessman, but I have long suspected that squalid dealings go on above that store of his."

The attorney concurred. "We have reason to believe that he has been in the slave business for twenty-five years, and we have identified eleven of his partners in crime. He has a strong grip over many Chinese in San Francisco. This girl's testimony combined with other evidence we already have may be enough to bring a guilty verdict to Wong She Duck."

Fierce Compassion

While Kwai Ying stayed at the home and gradually recovered, the government worked with Donaldina to build a strong case against Wong She Duck and his associates. Finally, in March 1935, over a year after Kwai Ying's escape, the respectable businessman Mr. Wong and two others were arrested. This news sent reverberations through Chinatown. Careful observers noticed the increased activity of messengers going in and out of tong headquarters, and prostitutes were bustled away in case of a raid. Chinatown was alert and tense.

It is the first day of the trial. I have lived in this home for more than one year and I wish I never had to leave. My friends smile their good wishes and pray for me. Lo Mo and Tien Wu walk closely by my side. They have not told me that I am in danger, but I know it very well. They surround me to show me that they will protect me.

I know that I must do this, and that if I fail, my life will be forfeit. If I fail, Lo Mo may have to return me to them. If the judge says that I can stay at the home, still they will hunt for me. They will not spare me.

We are at the courthouse now. It is so big and so cold. Then I see Wong She Duck, his wife, and the two other women. I remember that first day, when she pushed the coins in my hand and took them back again. I flinch. Lo Mo draws my hand through her arm. We practiced my testimony so many times, and yet I fear I will fail.

The judge says something in English that I cannot quite understand. I know what he is talking about, though; they told me what he would say. He is explaining the reason for this trial. He is charging them with the crime of transporting me illegally across borders and selling me against my will. There is no sound in this huge hall besides the judge's voice. Though there are many people in the room, always I am most aware of Wong She Duck and the others to my right. Their eyes see right into me.

I hear my name called. For a moment, I cannot walk, I cannot think, I cannot breathe. Then I look at Lo Mo. She gazes steadily at me and I

Justice

see confidence and love in her eyes. I walk to the witness stand and open my mouth. No sound comes out at first, but finally the words come. I tell my story, every shameful, degrading, humiliating part of it. Everything: dates, addresses, the day of my sale, and how the men took me, over and over, night after night. I keep my eyes locked on Lo Mo. Finally, that part is finished, but now comes the cross-examination.

Lo Mo explained to me that Wong She Duck is rich and can pay for a famous lawyer. This lawyer asks me questions and questions and more questions. Did you agree to come to America? Did anyone force you onto the ship? Did someone actually make you leave your homeland? So you chose to come to America? Now he talks to the jury. The translator explains some of it to me: My mind is inferior. I am merely a Chinese girl and could never have possibly remembered all of those details. I must have made them up. I am lying. No lower class, Chinese prostitute has a very good memory.

Wong She Duck is testifying now. He is very calm. Then many witnesses. He has hired these, Lo Mo warned me, to tell the jury of his good character as an honorable citizen and leader in the community.

After several days of intense pressure and questioning, Kwai Ying's fortitude crumbled. While standing in the witness box, her trembling hands covered her face to hide desperate tears.

The defense lawyer pounced, "See the girl? Her conscience has finally awakened. She was lying this whole time. Lying, I tell you!" Donaldina gripped her seat to keep herself from rushing up to Kwai Ying and taking her right back to 920. Why did she ever ask the poor girl to endure such a cunningly brutal ordeal?

The jury was dismissed for deliberation. Hours passed. Tension in the courtroom mounted. What could they be discussing?

Then they returned to give their verdict: Ten jurors asserted that Wong She Duck was guilty, but two contended for not guilty. The trial dissolved in a hung jury.

Fierce Compassion

Kwai Ying cried on Donaldina's shoulder as they drove home, hiding her face in shame. She had failed. Her new sisters at 920 were excited to greet her, but everyone's mood sunk to anxious gloom when they heard what had happened.

Three days after the trial's unhappy ending, a new hope glimmered. After a year of searching, the police had found and rescued another of Wong She Duck's slaves, a smart, tough woman named Wong So. Kwai Ying had earnestly hoped that this fellow slave would be saved before the trial, but until now, it had been to no avail.

Wong So joined the household at 920. She was bitter toward her abusers and eager to expose them. She had much evidence, and she seemed resilient and courageous. With Wong So by her side, Kwai Ying agreed to testify again. The trial was reopened.

Wong She Duck's lawyers had observed the influence that Donaldina Cameron and Tien Wu had on Kwai Ying, and secured orders to bar them both from the courtroom. Donaldina accepted this news grimly, saying simply, "There is One higher than I who will be present."

Wong So stood strong, firm and beautiful, answering each question with levelheaded determination. The newspapers loved the story. A headline in the *San Francisco Chronicle* read, "Huge Profit Made in Selling Girls," and thousands read about what was dubbed the "Broken Blossoms" case. Days passed and tension grew. Prayer was fervent.

Finally, the jury was again dismissed and again deliberated behind closed doors. This time, when they returned to the courtroom, they declared the defendants guilty. Wong She Duck, his wife, and one other partner would be fined and imprisoned. After they had served their terms, they would be deported.

Euphoria eruped at 920. Forgotten were cleaning and classes. The girls who had testified arrived home to joyful fanfare. Before that evening's dinner, the cacophony ceased for a minute. A hush fell over the room for a prayer of thanksgiving.

Justice

Through this trial, thirty slave traders were exposed, pointing a beam of piercing light into the darkness of the Chinese slave trade. The public was outraged about the atrocities of slavery in their midst. Other slaves heard of the demise of Wong She Duck and were emboldened to escape. Slave owners were deterred from continuing their business because of the increased risk of imprisonment and deportation.

While preparing for Wong She Duck's trial, Lo Mo celebrated her sixty-fifth birthday. She deflected suggestions for a big party. Instead, she wholeheartedly plunged into planning a memorable celebration for the sixtieth anniversary of the mission home. Many came from just down the street and from miles away to enjoy events that lasted three days. The highlight was a play titled "Sixty years, Sixty Minutes" that recounted the history of 920. Donaldina Cameron and Jack Manion played leading roles—as Donaldina Cameron and Jack Manion. It was the talk of the town.

Now, with both the trial and the sixtieth anniversary celebration successfully completed, it was time for Donaldina Cameron to face a new challenge. According to the rules of the mission board of the Presbyterian Church, it was time for her to retire. The indomitable Miss Cameron could barge into buildings full of violent criminals. She could witness confidently in court and convince police officers to do what she asked. She could speak eloquently to crowds. She managed a household of fifty and raised money for that household as well as other homes across the bay. She stayed up nights to tend the venereal sores of sick girls, and she graciously entertained important dignitaries. She interviewed her daughters' prospective husbands and threw smashing parties. Could she also retire?

The door through which Kwai Ying and so many others were invited into safety and new beginnings

Chapter Seventeen
The Rose of Palo Alto

Whom have I in heaven but you?
And earth has nothing I desire besides you.
My flesh and my heart may fail,
But God is the strength of my heart
And my portion forever.
Psalm 73:25-26

1952

"Tien, look at these exquisite roses. My favorite of all the wonders our Father has created in His kingdom of flowers."

"Yes, Lo Mo. Roses always were your favorite. And now you have a garden overflowing with them."

"Yes, Tien. Yes, I do." Donaldina Cameron was 83 years old. Her pure white hair was up in her signature bun, and her sharp, black, chiffon dress complemented her cheeks, which still showed hints of youthful pink. "Tien, when I die, I should like my friends to sing "Oh Love that Will Not Let Me Go," and I want only a few red roses to go with those last lines, "from the ground there blossoms red life that will endless be."

Donaldina Cameron in her Chinese silk. Used by permission of San Francisco History Center, San Francisco Public Library.

The Rose of Palo Alto

1939

Around Chinatown, slave trafficking and other crime was wilting. The profit was no longer worth the risk. Jackson Street, Ross Alley, Stockton, Kearney, Spofford, Waverly, Clay–all were safer. Indeed, the slave trade was so diminished that the national Presbyterian Mission board decided that it was no longer necessary to keep 920 as a women's safe house and decided instead to lease it to other organizations while the remaining staff and six residents rented a smaller space on Wetmore Street.

Oh, the life that had been lived this home: the tears and laughter, work and worship, birth and death, joy and devastating loss. How many hundreds, or thousands, of people counted this place as a vital, precious part of their lives? And now it was time to leave. Closets were emptied, personal belongings packed, decisions made about what to keep and what to leave behind. A mantle of sadness covered the home the day they moved. Donaldina walked through the hallways one more time, when the rooms had been emptied of everything but their memories. She prepared to hand over her ring of keys. "My blood is in the mortar of these bricks," she whispered, as she exited the oak door one last time.

Shortly after the mission home was leased, Donaldina Cameron left San Francisco. More than four decades after the young Dolly came to teach sewing for a year, she moved away–now as the beloved Lo Mo. Chinatown's most loved and most hated woman left her home knowing that this corner of the world had been radically transformed. She bid farewell with a promise to visit Chinatown soon and often. She arrived at the dock, mist swirling around her. A ferry brought her across the water to an apartment in Oakland, where she would live with her sisters Annie and Catharine.

1942

For the entirety of this book, we have fondly referred to the mission home as "920." The same home is today called Cameron House. It went against all of Donaldina's inclinations to allow the mission home to be named after her, and she objected at first, but eventually gave in; a good idea, since there was little she could do to prevent it. On June 7, 1942, the Presbyterian Occidental Mission Home was officially named the Donaldina Cameron House. It was a statement of hope for the future, since at that time the building was still being leased to other community groups.

Lo Mo, naturally, came to Chinatown for the renaming celebration. It was a joyful reunion. The now ancient T'sang T'sun, also known as Auntie Wing, sat in a place of honor, her presence a testimony to God's long faithfulness. She had been one of the first girls rescued by the mission when it started seventy years earlier, and had laid the cornerstone for the home in 1873 and again for the new building after the earthquake. Miss Donaldina Lew, one of many Chinatown citizens named after our heroine, sang for the dedication. Distinguished guest Sergeant Manion gave a moving speech detailing the immense pleasure he had taken in working alongside Miss Cameron. By the time that her old schoolmate Evelyn Browne Bancroft rose to read Scripture, Donaldina was not the only one with moist eyes.

1943

Donaldina and her sisters vacated their Oakland apartment and moved forty miles south of San Francisco to Palo Alto, close to their other sister, Jessie. Dolly and Annie lived in the little house and built a small redwood cottage on the property for Cathie and her seventeen cats. (It wasn't that Donaldina and Annie weren't fond of cats; they liked them very much, but not in such numbers.) Donaldina was known to sometimes sneak food to the poor mice as she encouraged them to escape from the jaws of her sister's cats. She also asked the man who delivered the vegetables to leave the tops on so she could share them with the cow across the street.

The three elderly Cameron sisters enthusiastically landscaped their new home. They lined the front walk with heather and Scottish broom and then christened their cottage "Heatherbroom." They planted three birches in the front yard and named one for each sister. They adorned the backyard with plants, juxtaposing a weeping willow with a prickly-branched pine. But the most striking feature about Heatherbroom was the rose garden. The shingled roof sloped down to a stone wall that barely peeked out from behind the thorny plants. After Donaldina had given it a few years of attention, a sea of roses threatened to drown the little cottage in waves of petals. Roses also lined the yard by the street, and soon the house became known as one of the sights of California Avenue. The scent of roses graced the inside of the house, as well, and visitors often left Heatherbroom laden with gifts of the fragrant blossoms.

Inside, a homey fireplace made a welcoming hearth for visitors. The walls of the living room were adorned with pictures of Scottish landscapes and the Cameron family as well as pictures of Chinese landscapes and her Chinese family. When letters arrived with photos, she found space for them on mantel and tables, and "cherubic Chinese babies smiled at dignified Old World Scots and American friends." Above the door to the hall was a plaque inscribed "Yet I Will Rejoice," from Donaldina's favorite Bible passage: "Though the fig tree does not bud and there are no grapes on the vines, though the olive crop fails and the fields produce no food, though there are no sheep in the pen and no cattle in the stalls, yet I will rejoice in the LORD, I will be joyful in God my Savior." The four short words on the plaque triggered many memories.

Donaldina often made the half-mile trek to J.J. & F's Market, trudging home with a full shopping bag. She showered her motherly instincts on any who found themselves in her path. One day as she enjoyed the smell of fresh bread in a bakery, she noticed that the salesgirl's hands were red and chapped. Donaldina took those cold hands and held them until they were warm. This would become a regular tradition; each time Donaldina walked to the bakery, the girl knew warmth in her frigid fingers.

Visitors came in multitudes during those first years of retirement, including journalists who knocked at the door in search of the captivating story of a Scottish woman with the gumption to face Chinatown's organized crime gangs. She tired of these interviews, and was known to hide when she saw reporters, shouting to her sisters, "The Philistines are coming!" Visits from children and their families were always welcome, however, and Donaldina's daughters and friends from Chinatown visited Lo Mo regularly, their boys and girls gathering around Miss Cameron's skirts and listening intently to the thrilling stories she told of evil and good, slaves and masters, kidnappings and rescues, and the love of God. Friends descended on Heatherbroom for holidays. Everyone seemed to love being in Miss Cameron's presence, and though her body grew weaker, her wit and charm never abandoned her, nor her ability to make others feel loved.

The sound of footsteps came up the walkway one afternoon. No curious reporter at the door this time, nor an old, familiar friend, but a dashing young Chinese man dressed in a crisp army uniform. Donaldina was startled to see him, until she recognized him as one of the boys she had taken to the Chung Mei Boys' Home a decade earlier. She invited him in, and she and Annie served him tea while he explained that he had come to say goodbye before he deployed to fight in World War II. More Chinese-American soldiers soon streamed to Heatherbroom on their way to the war, paying their respects to Lo Mo. These were orphans she had cradled as babies, or young men whom she had questioned intently before giving them their brides, or the sons of her daughters–her grandchildren and even great-grandchildren. Despite the decades of hostility and condescension they had experienced in their adopted homeland, many Chinese men still chose to fight for the United States. When America entered the war as an ally with China, the Chinese Exclusion Act, which had been consistently renewed since it was first enacted in 1882, became an embarrassment. In 1943, it was repealed.

A few of the soldiers who visited Donaldina also listed her as their next of kin. This meant other visits at the doorstep of Heatherbroom starting a few months later, deliveries of the dreaded telegrams that began, "We regret to inform you…"

After the war, Donaldina's sister Catharine left this world; three years later, Annie followed her, and finally Donaldina was the only one of seven Cameron siblings left. Tien Wu retired and moved into Catharine's little redwood cottage.

1960

After the war, the national Presbyterian mission board decided that there was again need for the building on Sacramento Street, and the Donaldina Cameron house was recommissioned. Thousands of Chinese refugees had begun arriving in San Francisco. Men could now bring their wives with them. Chinatown's quarters were exceedingly crowded. Racism remained, and new Cameron House director Lorna Logan observed that "The violence of the days of the Kearney riots has given place to a patronizing surface enthusiasm for the Chinese that just as firmly keeps them from living beyond the crowded confines of Chinatown, and from employment outside the Chinese community except as cooks." The Cameron House offered these new immigrants friendship and respect that went deeper than patronizing surface enthusiasm. Occasionally, the venerated Miss Cameron made the trip from Palo Alto to visit. All the activity of the home was called to a halt when this happened. Children and adults came together in the big gathering room, now called Culbertson Hall, and Lo Mo once again kept them spellbound with mesmerizing tapestries woven from threads of drama, humor, and the devoted love of God.

1967

"I did not want to live so long. Ninety-seven is a ghastly age," Donaldina wrote. "Age limitations are such a grievous hindrance—I cannot do for those I love the personal things that my heart prompts." But still she wrote letters, sent gifts to friends, encouraged her visitors, and rubbed cold hands. She was much loved, and on her ninety-eighth birthday, Heatherbroom could scarcely hold the flowers that arrived. Several months later, Donaldina fell and broke her hip. It did not heal, and she remained hospitalized. Friends noted that she ministered to hospital staff and visitors more than they to her.

January 4, 1968

Tien Wu sat by Donaldina's bed. They regularly shared a daily devotional together, and today's reading was a promise of Jesus in the gospel of John: "In My Father's house are many dwelling places; if it were not so, I would have told you; for I go to prepare a place for you. If I go and prepare a place for you, I will come again and receive you to Myself, that where I am, there you may be also."

Lo Mo talked to Tien about her joyous anticipation of being welcomed into that forever home.

Later that morning, Donaldina Mackenzie Cameron went to be with her Savior.

Chapter Eighteen
She Likes to Fly and Be Free
飛翔

*I sought the LORD, and he answered me;
he delivered me from all my fears.
Those who look to him are radiant;
their faces are never covered with shame.*
Psalm 34:4-5

*I have found that there are three stages
in every great work of God:
first, it is impossible, then it is difficult, then it is done.*
Hudson Taylor

"This way, hold my hand, the streets are crowded." We dodge around a crate full of winter melons and step onto Stockton Street. The melancholic sounds of the two-stringed erhu waft through the air from behind us, ambushing me with a flood of images, thoughts, memories. Searing pain, lonely shame. Anger, hatred, fear. My heart beats faster and I have to steady myself so that I do not flinch at every stranger who seems to look at me. Many times I have walked these streets as a free woman, yet fear still reaches for me like the hard hands of those who used to hurt me.

My daughter reaches up, "Hold me."

How can I say no to those sweet, imploring arms? I trudge up the steep hill, small girl against my chest.

Tears sting my eyes. "Here we are."

"This is where you lived?" Her face perks up and I set her down. She runs up the brick steps and stretches to knock on the door, the door of hope. As so many other girls have knocked before her.

Auntie Tien and Auntie Mae beam and chuckle, pinch my daughter's cheeks, ask if she is cold. Others come in and out of the hall. They are not surprised to see a guest, since the house is always busy. But it feels strange without Lo Mo. Auntie Tien takes my arm and leads us into the parlor for tea. We talk lightly of the past, of the happy days after the trial, and of the time my husband came to the house to court me. We talk of the present, of the problems of the new Chinese immigrants. Auntie Tien and Auntie Mae ask me all their questions and then they must return to work. They let me go to wander back through my memories.

Now we stand on a flat part of the roof of the home. The city of San Francisco spills out before me, so grand, stretching all the way to the patch of blue bay. Snatches of sound from the erhu vibrate up from the street once more. A melancholic melody, reminder of the sadness hidden in many corners of Chinatown. Sadness not only in Chinatown, but also in the rest of California, and America and China, and the world. But light shines into the darkness. Love pushes into the hidden shame and changes it.

Flags flutter from the tops of apartments and shops, declaring loyalty to Sun Yet Sen or Chiang Kai Shek, reminders of the fight leaders and political visions fighting for control of China. Times are changing. Shirts are strung across rooftop windows and stairways, clothes from Old China mingling with modern American fashions, a tapestry of two cultures meshed.

Cold fog has covered San Francisco for days and days. In the fog, everything looks strange. Familiar landscapes are shrouded in mist, concealing the buildings that you know are there. It reminds me now of something I once heard Lo Mo say. I practiced repeating it over and over to remember until I could write it carefully down. "God's Providences are written in letters of gold across the months, dim sometimes through the mist of tears, but never quite hidden."

Remembering my past is like looking through fog. Through the mist, I see the man talking to my mother, giving her money while I watch from the corner. Hong Kong becomes smaller as the ship moves out into the ocean, away from everything I know. I am nervous but happy, excited for my future. That feeling is difficult to remember. When I look back, I see a naïve, uneducated girl. The old Kwai Ying is gone. I have suffered so much since then that it is almost as if I were a different person.

I try not to remember what comes next. But sometimes the memories come into my dreams, riding on waves of shame and fear, and I wake up feeling sick and hopeless. I sit in the dark until I remember who I am, the new Kwai Ying, with a loving husband, a beautiful daughter, a church where I learn to know and serve the God who rescued me. Kwai Ying, who can choose to spend a day visiting her old home without fear of being caught and beaten.

This afternoon, wind has pushed away the cloud and fog, and the sun has broken through. I gaze over Chinatown, gleaming after all of the wet. I have forgotten about my companion here on the roof, but now I look at her. She is studying the little pots of herbs that soak in the sun. She says their names in Cantonese: jan sam, gan cao, sheng jiang. But she counts them in English: one, two three. Her bangs fall into her face as she concentrates. She has her father's gentle eyes.

How can it be that I am mother to such a beautiful girl, and wife to a fine man? I ache with the goodness of it.

"Mama," she says. She stops counting and looks over the roofs with me. "Tell me about the time Lo Mo brought you here on the roof and showed you the whole city and told you about Jesus."

Fierce Compassion

Oh, Lo Mo, I miss you. But your spirit is here and will never leave. This is the most precious place in the world.

My little girl does not wait for me to answer the first question before asking another, "Mama, did she really walk across the roofs wearing a disguise so she could find girls like you?"

I brush a piece of dirt off her dress. I am about to tell her again the stories she loves to hear when we see it together. A tiny bird. A hummingbird in Chinatown! How brave, to come here despite the big, fat pigeons and the crowds and the cement and brick, and with so few of the flowers that hummingbirds love. The delicate bird is so small, and she flies so quickly. We watch her hover over the garlic blossom. Her green wings shimmer like satin, a white collar encircles her violet throat, and her wings go so fast we can hardly see them.

She flits, flits, flits, among the flowers in the herb garden, and then suddenly flies up and away, into the bright blue sky, up until we cannot see her.

We are quiet for a moment, holding hands, and then my little girl speaks in reverent hush, "She likes to fly and be free, Mama."

"Yes. Yes, she does, Donaldina."

Donaldina Cameron in 1960 at the age of 91

Is It True?

Dear Readers,

As you perused this text, you may have wondered what of the stories, dialogue, and characters is strict historical fact and what is elaboration. Well, in case you were wondering, this book is a result of thorough research that ignited our imagination.

The stories are true. All of those girls and women really were rescued. Donaldina really did miss a meeting with President Wilson. There were little girls named Tien Wu and Flora Wong. The dramatic twists in the trials of Kum Qui and Kwai Ying were as we recorded them—including Donaldina Cameron being pushed onto a Palo Alto road in the middle of the night. After the earthquake struck San Francisco, Donaldina really did disregard the soldier who threatened to shoot her. It is also most earnestly recorded by a witness of the time that she did in fact heave a stone onto the head of an unsuspecting cow who was mistaken for a sinister intruder. The more outrageous-sounding narratives are the most likely to be painstakingly accurate. We only filled in the more mundane details.

There is but one story in which it might be wise to call into question some of the details; that is the story of Mae in Chapter 15. We took it from Mildred Martin's accurate biography of Donaldina Cameron (*Chinatown's Angry Angel*), but she took her details from a more florid book called *The Ways of Ah Sin: A Composite Narrative of Things As They Are* by Donaldina's friend and ally Charles Shepherd, and we cannot entirely vouch for his accuracy; he may have pieced together particulars of this story from multiple rumors that he heard. Regardless, we do know that the essentials of this event took place. Louie Sam, a hatchetman, rescued his sister at the expense of his life.

Not all of the words Donaldina Cameron says in the book were transcribed verbatim, although as often as possible we crafted portions of dialogue directly from words that we know she said. We took liberties with some of her written words by placing them in different settings. To help us make invented dialogue more genuine, we immersed ourselves in books written during the time of Donaldina Cameron so that we could incorporate that era's colloquialisms.

Did we sometimes add sensory details to enhance the plot and make it more real? Yes, we did, although not without careful consideration. Do we know if they laughed at their Thanksgiving party? Well, no, but one can guess. We do know that Donaldina did have a turkey carving contest with her guest! Some of the details from Dolly's childhood came from our imaginations, as there is little recorded about this time of her life. Her mother died when Dolly was five, but we don't know if the little girl ran to a field of wildflowers to lament. Her father's sheep were stolen and killed before his eyes, but we don't know if he gathered his children around the fireplace to tell them of the calamity.

We have read so much about Donaldina Cameron, and talked to as many as we could find who knew her or knew of her, that as we wrote, we became convinced that we knew this woman without having yet met her.

We hope that any minor additions we have made are not far from the truth, and we hope that you have enjoyed the book.

Sincerely yours,
K & K Wong

Kathryn and Kristin Wong at the door of Cameron House

The Cameron House Today
by Doreen Der-McLeod

In 1943 the "Mission Home" was renamed Cameron House in honor of Donaldina Cameron, the woman who spent 40 years advocating and caring for the women and girls she rescued. Although Cameron House no longer provides shelter and housing, it continues to be a place of safety, help, and healing for those who enter the heavy wooden doors where dynamite had once been planted.

Today, the doors are no longer guarded and locked, but can be open by both young and old, who come to Cameron House for a multitude of services. The building resounds with the footsteps or excited voices of those who are part of its many activities. Over a thousand persons are served each year through social services, youth programs, educational workshops, leadership training and advocacy. Of these, 400 are children and youth who benefit from afterschool tutorial, Friday night Club Program, Summer Daycamp, and/or the Bilingual Summer Youth Program. The summer leadership program trains 80 High school volunteers to work with children.

Bilingual and bicultural Social Service staff provides linguistic and cultural sensitive counseling for Cantonese and Mandarin clients. They provide one of two existing Cantonese language cancer support groups in San Francisco for those isolated by their diagnosis of cancer. In the past two decades, the Social Service Department has worked collaboratively with Asian Pacific Islander Legal Outreach, Asian Women Shelter and Narika to provide seamless services to victims of domestic violence. More recently, this collaboration also assists men and women trafficked to the United States for cheap labor or prostitution. As in Miss Cameron's time, staff today continue to help immigrants in transitioning to life in America through English classes or through accessing resources for housing, employment, educational or medical needs.

The legacy of love and care for those who are victimized continues in the work of Cameron House today. It is an agency that has historically developed indigenous leadership. Cameron House alumni provide leadership in city agencies, non-profits, the Presbyterian Church and Cameron House itself. Many of the Cameron House staff are former participants from its youth programs. Here they learned that God's caring extends to all of us. They experience community, and are taught the value of giving back to the community. As with many who passed through those heavy wooden door during Miss Cameron's time, the love and care a new generation receives at this place called "920", transforms their lives and allows them to develop their full potential.

Cameron House represents 137 years of unbroken service to Chinatown and to Asians throughout San Francisco. It maintains the tradition of serving those in need and remains a beacon of hope,

The work of Cameron House is rooted and inspired by the courage and sacrifice of those early missionary women—Miss Culbterson, Miss Cameron, Miss Higgins and the girls they rescued, Ah Cheng, Tien Wu, and Mae Wong, who joined in the rescue work. The story of the Mission Home continues today with a new generation of immigrants who have come to the "Gold Mountain" for greater opportunity, and for the grandchildren of those women and girls rescued by Miss Cameron who now comprise the third or fourth generation of Chinese in America.

Doreen Der-McLeod was a participant in Cameron House youth programs and served as the Executive Director of Cameron House from 2000-2009.

Slavery Today

Margaret Culbertson passed the baton to Donaldina Cameron who now passes it to us. In many ways, slavery today is strikingly similar to the slavery of Donaldina Cameron's day. Girls and young women are tricked, coerced, or kidnapped, and then brought to foreign lands with unfamiliar streets and strange languages. They are stripped of their passports, their confidence, their dignity, and their humanity. They become merchandise to be purchased. This happens far away in places like Asia and Europe. It also happens very, very close, in our own country and states and cities and neighborhoods.

Experts debate the number of people currently enslaved in the world today. Estimates range from 12 million to 27 million people. According to the U.S. State Department, between 14,500 and 17,500 people are trafficked into the United States every year from other countries. This does not include those trafficked within our own borders. The average age of entry into prostitution in the United States is 12-14 years old, and between 100,000 and 300,000 children in America are at risk for sex trafficking each year. But it is impossible to pin down specific numbers when so many of these victims are hidden and voiceless.

In the process of writing this book, we tried to estimate how many people are alive in the world today because of Donaldina Cameron. Many teenagers who came to the home would otherwise have suffered early, lonely deaths. Because of the boldness and perseverance of Donaldina and those who worked with her, hundreds of these women instead married and had their own children, who then had their own children, and grandchildren…We gave up trying to count.

Donaldina Cameron's life has changed the world forever. We reach out with hope and expectation to take the baton from her hand. What does it mean to run this race after her? It might start with saying "yes" to a request to teach sewing for a year.

More information on modern day slavery

U.S. State Department Trafficking in Persons Report 2010
www.state.gov/documents/organization/142979.pdf

In the United States: Hope House

In the beauty and calm of the mountains of western North Carolina sits a home that on the outside looks to be nothing unique or unusual. But in reality, within the walls of this particular home, young adolescent girls experience for the first time something they never thought possible: Hope.

In the United States there is a lack of safe shelter for women and girls who have been victims of trafficking, and who have specialized needs for restoration of body, mind, and soul.

Hope House is a faith-based home of seclusion, restoration, and healing for domestic victims of sex trafficking. It offers long-term shelter for victims ages 12-17 and a transitional living program for victims ages 18-25.

"God has shown me that the most shattered, battered, and broken people still stand a chance, I can be saved. I always looked at myself as if I was a failure, a waste of life... I never knew that there were people out there who would love & care for me the way they did."
–16 year old trafficking survivor.

www.hopehousenc.com

In Cambodia: Transitions Global

Every girl is sacred. Every girl deserves dignity.
Every girl needs a dream. And no girl should ever be sold.

Transitions provides comprehensive restorative aftercare for girls rescued from sex trafficking. Each girl at Transitions receives personalized care to heal her past and provide opportunities for her future. A girl who finds her home at Transitions finds a new beginning. She finds hope, and with holistic trauma therapy, life skills and sustainable career training, she finds a dream for her future.

At Transitions we believe every girl in our program deserves the highest level of dignity and opportunity we can provide. We also believe every girl is capable of achieving her dreams with the right support and encouragement. We don't allow girls to settle for what society has told them they are capable of, like sewing and handycrafts; we know they can do so much more.

Every girl in our program studies English and computer technology and then goes on to find her dream. Shine Career School provides a firsthand opportunity to train girls in any career field they choose, and will serve to overcome the gap in training choices, by providing a high quality learning environment. Shine will facilitate teaching opportunities for professionals around the world, in a variety of fields, to come to Cambodia and teach, while empowering survivors with the skills and knowledge they need to take control of their lives.

www.transitionsglobal.org

Around the World: International Justice Mission

Our Vision: To rescue thousands, protect millions and prove that justice for the poor is possible.

International Justice Mission is a human rights agency that brings rescue to victims of slavery, sexual exploitation and other forms of violent oppression. IJM lawyers, investigators and aftercare professionals work with local officials to secure immediate victim rescue and aftercare, to prosecute perpetrators and to ensure that public justice systems - police, courts and laws - effectively protect the poor.

IJM's justice professionals work in their communities in 13 countries in Asia, Africa and Latin America to secure tangible and sustainable protection of national laws through local court systems.

www.ijm.org

> *No fiction is half so incredible as the story of what God can do with plain, ordinary women when they let him have His way in their lives.*
> Hallie Winsborough, First Secretary of Woman's Work the Presbyterian Church in the United States.

Timeline

Chinese and American History

1849
The American Gold Rush begins

1861-1865
The American Civil War

1869
The completion of the transcontinental railroad

1874
The Presbyterian Mission Home opens in San Francisco

1875
The Page Act begins Chinese exclusion

1882
The Chinese Exclusion Act

The Life of Donaldina Cameron

July 26, 1869
Donaldina Cameron is born

1874
Isabella Cameron dies

1882
The Camerons move to Oakland

1888
Allan Cameron dies

Donaldina's engagement to George Sargent

1895
Donaldina comes to 920

1897
Miss Culbertson dies

1898
Donaldina becomes superintendent of 920

1900 Bubonic plague scare in San Francisco **1900** Boxer Rebellion in China protesting foreign influence	**1900** Yuen Qui dies and a lifelong friendship is forged between Miss Cameron and Tien Wu. **1901** Kum Qui's rescue Teddy Roosevelt visits 920 **1904** Donaldina falls in love with Charles Bazata **1905** Donaldina goes on sabbatical
1906 The San Francisco Earthquake & Fire	**1906** The San Francisco Earthquake, 920 destroyed by dynamite **1908** Dedication of the New 920
1911 The overthrow of the Manchurian Dynasty	**1911** Donaldina's engagement to Nathaniel Tooker **1915** The Tooker Memorial Home is opened **1916** Allan Cameron's death

1917
The United States joins WWI

1918
Influenza epidemic

1919
Charles Shepherd comes to San Francisco

1920
Twenty-fifth anniversary of Donaldina's work

1921
Jack Manion comes to Chinatown

1929
The stock markets crash and the Great Depression begins

1931
The Japanese invade China

1933
The Broken Blossoms Case begins

1934
Sixtieth anniversary of the Home and Donaldina's sixty-fifth birthday

1935
The Broken Blossoms Case is won

1938
Lorna Logan officially records the "end of the slave traffic"

1941
Donaldina moves to Palo Alto

1941
The United States enters WWII

1941
920 named the Donaldina Cameron House

1945-1949
The Japanese invade China

January 4, 1968
Donaldina Cameron dies

Notes on Quotations:
Who Inspired Donaldina Cameron?

The quotations at the beginning of the chapters of this book were written by some whom we suspect that Donaldina Cameron would have read for encouragement and fellowship. These were stalwart men and women whose company we think she would have much enjoyed.

Above all, every day, Donaldina read her Bible. Its insistent themes of evil and good, of justice and of God's advocacy for the downtrodden would have leaped out to her as immediately relevant. Though she most likely read the King James translation, we have chosen to take most verses from the New International Version to highlight their relevance to this generation.

JOHN BUNYON (1628-1688) is best known as the author of *Pilgrim's Progress*. He lived in a time of religious upheaval in England. During periods of relative religious freedom, he was a popular preacher; other times he was imprisoned because of his persistence in preaching without a license. Twelve years in jail gave him time to write *Pilgrim's Progress* and many other works. The pilgrimage of Christian was filled with despondency, vanity, doubt, and attack from evil men and was surely heartening for Donaldina and her household of women on the path from slavery to freedom.

AMY CARMICHAEL (1867-1951) an Irish Presbyterian, was born 18 months before Donaldina Cameron, and sailed to India the same year that Dolly went to San Francisco. Both of them spent their lives serving girls and women who had been rescued from forced prostitution. Like Donaldina, Amy had stalwart courage and conviction, as well as strong relational and administrative gifts that helped her run a large household. Her daughters called her "Amma" as Donaldina's called her "Lo Mo." Like Donaldina, Amy was thought too radical by some of her countrymen of the time, and like Donaldina, she never married. Surely Miss Cameron and Miss Carmichael would have enjoyed long conversations together. Amy Carmichael wrote over thirty books, popular among Christians of the time, and it is likely that Donaldina was encouraged by her work.

OTIS GIBSON (1826-1889) was a Methodist minister and stalwart defender of the Chinese in San Francisco during the tumultuous 1870s. He was a missionary in China for ten years before returning to the U.S., where he became a staunch advocate for the Chinese community in a time of rabid racism. He wrote *The Chinese in America* to try to interpret and explain his Chinese friends to his American countrymen. In 1877, he risked his life to protect Chinese while rioters were hunting for victims.

ANNE STEELE (1716-1778) was an English hymn writer. When she was three, her mother died. When she was 19 years old, she injured her hip, making her an invalid the rest of her life. Two years later, on the day before her wedding, her fiancé drowned. She wrote poetry and hymns under the pen-name of Theodosia, donating the proceeds to charity, and she helped her father in his pastoral work. She was bedridden for the last nine years of her life, but her disposition was described as cheerful and her life as one of "unaffected humility, warm benevolence, sincere friendship, and genuine devotion."

HARRIET BEECHER STOWE (1811-1896) was the American abolitionist best known as the author of the controversial *Uncle Tom's Cabin*, which captured the country's attention and pushed forward the discussion about slavery. She was nurtured in a large family that valued education for girls; her sister Catharine was a pioneer of women's education, and another sister Isabella helped start the National Women's Suffrage Association. (Donaldina also had sisters named Catharine and Isabella!) Harriet traveled around the country speaking on progressive ideas. She wrote that, "'I feel now that the time is come when even a woman or a child who can speak a word for freedom and humanity is bound to speak... I hope every woman who can write will not be silent."

HUDSON TAYLOR (1832-1905) sailed from England to China at the age of 21 and spent the rest of his life in arduous pioneer missionary work for the Chinese. He broke with conventions of the time, giving up many British traditions in order to identify with the Chinese. He learned several dialects of Chinese, wore Chinese clothing, and even grew a long braid. He started the China Inland Mission and recruited scores of missionaries to join him.

WILLIAM WILBERFORCE (1759-1833) was a British Member of Parliament who declared that God had given him two life goals: the abolition of the British slave trade and the reformation of British moral life. He was a winsome speaker and devout Christian whose persevering work eventually resulted in the abolition of the slavery throughout the British Empire.

Index of Chinese Characters

陷阱	Cage	拯救	Rescue
掏金	Gold	堅忍	Perseverance
成長	Grow	信仰	Faith
恐懼	Fear	博愛	Love
憐憫	Mercy	友愛	Brotherly Love
老母	Lo Mo	友情	Friendship
果決	Resolute	正義	Justice
盼望	Hope	天國	Kingdom of Heaven
家園	Home	飛翔	Fly

NOTES

We have relied heavily on *Chinatown Quest* by Carol Green Wilson (1932) and *Chinatown's Angry Angel* by Mildred Martin (1977) and have not specifically cited every instance that we have drawn from their detailed accounts.

Chapter 2: Gold

21 Part of the Promontory Summit prayer, offered by Reverend Todd of Massachusetts: "God of Creation and God of Providence, thou hast created the heavens and the earth, the valleys and the hills… We rejoice that thou hast created the human mind with its power of invention, its capacity of expansion, and its guardian of success. We have assembled here this day, upon the height of the continent, from varied sections of our country, to do homage to thy wonderful name, in that thou hast brought this mighty enterprise, combining the commerce of the east with the gold of the west to so glorious a completion." (Central Pacific Railroad Photographic History Museum)

22 During the peak of the most grueling work, Chinese laborers made up ninety percent of the Central Pacific's work force. More about the railroad and the Promontory Summit ceremony can be found in Chang *The Chinese in America*; Ambrose, *Nothing Like It In the World*; and the online Central Pacific Railroad Photographic History Museum.

22 In gold mining camps, "the Chinaman was welcomed as long as the surface gold was plentiful enough to make rich all who came. But that happy situation was not long to continue…California did not fulfill the promise of the golden tales that had been told of her. These gold-seekers were disappointed. In the bitterness of their disappointment they turned upon the men of other races who were working side by side with them and accused them of stealing their wealth. They boldly asserted that California's gold belonged to them. The cry of 'California for the Americans' was raised and taken up on all sides. Within a short time the Frenchman, the Mexican and the Chileño had been driven out and the full force of this anti-foreign persecution fell upon the unfortunate Chinaman." (Norton, *The Story of California From the Earliest Days to the Present.*)

23 "a race of people": The People of the State of California v. George W. Hall. In this case, George Hall, a white man, was tried and convicted of murdering Ling Sing, a Chinese miner. The principal witnesses were three other Chinese men. The sentence was overturned (and Mr. Hall was freed), when it was determined that evidence from Chinese witnesses was not admissible.

23 "the settlement among us of an inferior race": Leland Stanford inauguration speech from Central Pacific Railroad Photographic Historic Museum and Logan, *Ventures in Mission*.

23 "Vast pool of cheap, plentiful and easily exploitable labor," and other details about Chinese work on the railroads: Chang, *The Chinese in America* and Young, *The Transcontinental Railroad*.

24 Details of Donaldina Cameron's birth and travel to San Francisco: Wilson, *Chinatown Quest* and Martin, *Chinatown's Angry Angel*. Donaldina's family remembers her fascination watching the Chinese men from the hotel window.

26 Prayer on the golden spike: Central Pacific Railroad Photographic History Museum

Chapter 3: Growing Pains

30 Perhaps that is how it was on the spring day when Isabella Cameron died, though we do not know the details. Donaldina Cameron kept parts of her life private. And Dolly was young enough when Isabella Cameron died that memories of her mother became faint. But all the Cameron children grew up insisting that there was no one so lovely as their gentle Scottish mother. Details of the Cameron family life and ranch from *Chinatown Quest* and *Chinatown's Angry Angel*.

32 Historian John Higham claims that "No variety of anti-European sentiment has ever approached the violent extremes to which anti-Chinese agitation went in the 1870s and 1880s. Lynching, boycotts, and mass expulsions…harassed the Chinese." (*Strangers in the Land* 25). A San Francisco resident observed that: "In 1852 the Chinamen were allowed to turn out and celebrate the Fourth of July and it was considered a happy time. In 1862 they would have been mobbed. In 1872 they would have been burned at the stake." (Dillon, *Hatchet Men* 54)

32	The Page Act's stated goal was to keep prostitutes out of the country, but zealous enforcement led to nearly all Chinese women being barred from entry. Seven years after the Page Act was passed, nearly 40,000 Chinese entered the United States; only 136 of these were women. The full text of the Page Act can be found at the University of California Hastings College of Law.
32	Senator George Frisbie Hoar of Massachusetts, who opposed the Exclusion Act, called it "nothing less than the legalization of racial discrimination." (Daniels, *Coming to America* 271)
33	According to the 1880 census, San Francisco's Chinese population consisted of 71,244 men and 3,888 women. (Dillon, *Hatchet Men*)
33	The Chinese cultural view of women combined with severe economic stress made some parents willing to sell their daughters. According to commentators of the time, many Chinese peasants did not think that women had souls (Corbett, *Poker Bride* 45). Girls also did not bring economic help to families, since they left their fathers' households when they married.
34	"Most Chinese prostitutes": In the 1870s, a girl could be bought in China for as low as $50 and sold in San Francisco for as much as $1000. Details about Chinese prostitution from Yung *Unbound Feet* 27-30 and notes for page 37.
36	Details about the dedication of Presbyterian mission home from Logan, *Ventures in Mission*.

Chapter 4: The Terror of Chinatown

39	"It is a humiliating fact": Otis Gibson, *The Chinese in America* 293, quoted in Chi, *Glimmers of Light* 33.
41	Tien Wu's sale, slavery, and rescue is told in Wilson, *Chinatown Quest* and Martin, *Chinatown's Angry Angel*.
41	Advertisement from a 19th century circular posted by a Hong Kong brokerage office in the Pearl River delta, cited in Corbett, *Poker Bride* 15.

41   Phrasebook: *Poker Bride* 15-16 and Moyers, *Becoming American: The Chinese Experience*

42   Chinese civic groups were organized by the provinces in China from which their members came, and were together called the Six Companies, after the six regions in Canton which sent the most immigrants to America. The Six Companies filled multiple roles: court to mediate disputes, diplomatic office to deal with the American world outside, and social aid society to relieve Chinatown's poverty. Affiliation with the Six Companies was an important part of survival in America.

43   "They are the terror of Chinatown": One investigator studying the tongs in San Francisco's Chinatown during the 1880s concluded, "the power of the highbinder tongs against the Chinese population is almost absolute. So great is the dread inspired among the Chinese by these societies that few have the courage to resist their criminal demands." Quotes and information about the tongs from Dillon *The Hatchet Men*, including 34, 54, 203.

43   "tall, handsome, dignified": Chang, *The Chinese in America*.

44   "ground between the hoodlums": Dillon *The Hatchet Men*

44   It must be noted that San Francisco at this time was known as wild and lawless, lacking the moral restraints of the east, and that there were many white prostitutes as well. But Chinese and Latin American prostitutes were singled out in American popular opinion as being particularly worthy of moral condemnation. (Yung *Unbound Feet* 31).

45   Stories of the early years of the mission home from Logan *Ventures in Mission* 9-12

48   "My darling sister": Letter and other details from Dolly's youth from Martin, *Chinatown's Angry Angel*

Chapter 6: Passing the Baton

62   *Book of Common Prayer*, Family Prayer, "In the Morning."

63   "Another method of torture": Transcribed from the "Register of Inmates"

66 "Some of the newly rescued girls": Donaldina Cameron in Women's Occidental Board of Foreign Missions Annual Reports 1874-1920.

69 "our valued assistant": Margaret Culbertson in Women's Occidental Board of Foreign Missions Annual Reports 1874-1920.

Chapter 7: Life and Death in a New Century

73 Public kissing on New Year's Eve 1899: *Nation's Business*, January 1900.

74 "Instead of fireworks, gunfire rang": Chase, *Barbary Plague* 15.

74 "filled with dread": San Francisco politicians considered moving all the Chinese to Angel Island. Chinatown rested on prime San Francisco real estate, and some would have been glad to take advantage of the plague infection to claim the property for other purposes. Some in Chinatown thought that the plague was a hoax, invented by greedy racist whites as excuse for another bout of painful discrimination. Fear of plague, fear of job loss, fear of starvation, fear of being forced from their homes: "The Chinese were sick with dread." This and other plague details from Chase *Barbary Plague*

80 *San Francisco Chronicle* 3 April 1900.

84 "her memory will be": Donaldina Cameron in Women's Occidental Board of Foreign Missions Annual Reports 1874-1920.

Chapter 8: Of Love and Travel and the Like

93 Sir Ewen Cameron great-great-grandfather of David Cameron: Wikipedia "Sir Ewen Cameron"

Chapter 9: Family Scrapbook

106 "Strength in need, counselor in perplexity, comfort in sorrow, and companion in joy" is from the marriage prayer in the *Book of Common Prayer*

106 "With the past year literally filled": and other quotations from this chapter: Donaldina Cameron in Women's Occidental Board of Foreign Missions Annual Reports 1874-1920.

Chapter 10: Though the Earth Give Way

Details and quotations in this chapter are taken from Donaldina' Cameron's account of the earthquake written for the Women's Occidental Board of Foreign Missions Annual Reports and recorded also in the Virtual Museum of the City of San Francisco article "Donaldina Cameron's Account of the Flight from Chinatown." sfmuseum.net

115 Looting of Chinatown: Chang, *The Chinese in America*

115 Sources rank the earthquake and fire one of the country's top five worst natural disasters, based on estimated number of deaths.

Chapter 11: The New 920

124 Samples of poetry and other information about the history of Angel Island at the Angel Island Immigration Station Foundation. aiisf.org

124 Tye Leung's story from Yung, *Unbound Voices* and *More Than Petticoats: Remarkable California Women* by Erin Turner

Chapter 12: Nathaniel

129 Quotations from Donaldina's speech taken from Women's Occidental Board of Foreign Missions Annual Reports

Chapter 14: Mae and Manion

147 Mae's story is taken from *The Ways of Ah Sin*, written by Donaldina Cameron's colleague Charles Shepherd, who called it "a compositve narrative of the way things are." It is not clear from his account which details were factually tied to these particular people and events and which were taken from other incidents or embellished.

152 "Greater love hath no one than this": John 15:13

Chapter 15: Allies Near and Far

162 "The name of Ah-Peen Oie": *Chinatown Quest* 110

166 "There came a man sent from God": John 1:6

Chapter 16: Justice

169 "whether a tie resulted": *Chinatown's Angry Angel* 251

171 "Oh, I like to live in this home": from Josephine Chi 24, taken from Donaldina Cameron "Stories of Rescue" Brochure from Occidental Board Mission Home for Chinese Girls, 1920, Bancroft Historical Library, University of California at Berkeley

Chapter 17: The Rose of Palo Alto

183 "Cherubic Chinese babies": *Chinatown's Angry Angel* 286

183 "Though the fig tree does not bud": Habakkuk 3:17-18

185 "The violence of the days": Lorna Logan in *Chinatown's Angry Angel* 272

186 "In My Father's House": John 14:1-3

BIBLIOGRAPHY
And some recommendations for further reading

Donaldina Cameron

We are indebted to the two authors who were the first caretakers of many of the stories in this book. Their enthusiastic and thorough writing paved the way for this book. Carol Green Wilson, one of Donaldina Cameron's many friends, approached her with the idea of writing a biography. Donaldina repeatedly said no: She did not want much made of her. Finally she relented, with the condition that the book emphasize the team nature of the mission. Once permission was granted, the author faced the challenge of catching the busy Donaldina Cameron long enough to collect material. We are glad that she persevered. Wilson's *Chinatown Quest* was published in 1932. Three decades later, freelance writer Mildred Crowl Martin was given the assignment of interviewing the octogenarian Donaldina Cameron. Full of trepidation (she had heard that Donaldina disliked reporters), she knocked on the door of the cottage in Palo Alto, and was soon drinking tea and falling under Lo Mo's gracious spell. She wrote the article and came back for more, devoting several years before and after Lo Mo's death to research and writing. *Chinatown's Angry Angel* was published in 1977. Mildred Crowl Martin donated audiotapes, correspondence, ideas, and drafts to Stanford University, where we spent happy days retracing her steps. Readers who want to discover the stories we had to leave out may enjoy reading these earlier biographies.

The Chinese in America

To understand the complex interplay of culture and history that contributed to Chinese slavery in the United States, we recommend *The Chinese in America* by Iris Chang and *Unbound Feet: A Social History of Chinese Women in San Francisco* by Judy Yung. Also helpful is the Bill Moyers PBS series *Becoming American*.

Modern Slavery

It has been important to us to connect issues of slavery and women's oppression of the last century with issues of slavery and women's oppression today. For this, we recommend *Half the Sky: Turning Oppression into Opportunity for Women Worldwide* by Nicholas Kristof and Sheryl WuDunn and *Half the Church: Recapturing God's Global Vision for Women* by Carolyn Custis James.

Fiction, and for young readers

Sold by Patricia McCormick is the gripping fictional account of a girl sold into slavery in modern India.

Paper Daughter by Jeannette Ingold, is a young adult story narrated by a winsome Chinese-American young writer trying to understand her heritage.

Many books for children and youth by Laurence Yep show the historical challenges of the Chinese in America.

Selected Bibliography

Abrams, Kerry. "Polygamy, Prostitution, and the Federalization of Immigration Law." Rev. of The Page Act. Columbia Law Review Apr. 2005: 641-716.

Ambrose, Stephen E. *Nothing like It in the World: the Men Who Built the Transcontinental Railroad, 1863-1869*. New York: Simon & Schuster, 2000.

Becoming American: The Chinese Experience. Bill Moyers. PBS, 2003. DVD.

"Chinese-American Contribution to the Transcontinental Railroad." Central Pacific Railroad Photographic History Museum - Transcontinental Railroad.

California Historical Society. www.californiahistoricalsociety.org

Chang, Iris. *The Chinese in America: a Narrative History*. New York: Viking, 2003.

Chase, Marilyn. *The Barbary Plague: the Black Death in Victorian San Francisco*. New York: Random House, 2003. Print.

Chi, Josephine. "Glimmers of Light Amidst the Darkness: The Untold Story of Missionaries and Chinese Christians in San Francisco from 1850 to 1920." A senior essay in history and East Asian studies. Berkeley College of Yale University, 1994.

Corbett, Christopher. *The Poker Bride: The First Chinese in the Wild West*. New York, NY: Atlantic Monthly, 2010.

Daniels, Roger. *Coming to America: A History of Immigration and Ethnicity in American Life*. New York, NY: HarperCollins, 1990.

Dillon, Richard H. *The Hatchet Men: The Story of the Tong Wars in San Francisco's Chinatown*. New York: Coward-McCann, 1962.

"Doreen Der-McLeod Interview." Personal interview. 17 Aug. 2010.

Genthe, Arnold and John Kuo Wei Tchen. *Genthe's Photographs of San Francisco's Old Chinatown*. New York: Dover Publications, 1984.

The Gold Rush. PBS: Alexandria, VA. 2006. Video.

The Great San Francisco Earthquake. Perf. F. Murray Abraham. PBS, 2005. DVD.

"Harry Chuck Interview." Personal interview. 20 Aug. 2010.

Higham, John. *Strangers in the Land: Patterns of American Nativism, 1860-1925*. New York: Atheneum, 1963. Print.

Ingold, Jeanette. *Paper Daughter*. Boston: Houghton Mifflin Harcourt, 2010. Print.

"Jeanette Wei Interview." Personal interview. 17 Aug. 2010.

Jennings, Dean S. "Smashing California's Yellow Slave Traffic." *True Magazine*. January 1936.

Kristof, Nicholas and Sheryl WuDunn, *Half the Sky: Turning Oppression into Opportunity for Women Worldwide*. New York: Alfred A. Knopf, 2009.

Library of Congress, "The Chinese in California, 1850-1925."

Ling, Huping. "Family and Marriage of Late-Nineteenth and Early-Twentieth Century Chinese Immigrant Women." *Journal of American Ethnic History 19.2 (2000)*: 43. InfoTrac U.S. History Collection.

Logan, Lorna. *Ventures in Mission: The Cameron House Story*. Wilson Creek, Washington: Crawford Hobby Print Shop, 1976.

Magagnini, Stephen, "Chinese Transformed 'Gold Mountain." *The Sacramento Bee*, 18 Jan 1998.

Martin, Mildred Crowl. *Chinatown's Angry Angel: The Story of Donaldina Cameron*. Palo Alto, CA: Pacific, 1977.

McCunn, Ruthanne Lum. *Thousand Pieces of Gold: a Biographical Novel*. Boston: Beacon, 1988.

Museum of the City of San Francisco. www.sfmuseum.org

Natale, Valerie. "Angel Island: 'Guardian of the Western Gate" Department of English, College of LAS, University of Illinois.

Norton, Henry. "Gold Rush and Anti-Chinese Race Hatred - 1849." Museum of the City of San Francisco.

Norton, Henry. *The Story of California from the Earliest Days to the Present*. Chicago: A.C. McClurg &, 1913.

Pascoe, Peggy. *Relations of Rescue: The Search for Female Moral Authority in the American West, 1875-1939*. New York: Oxford University Press, 1990.

Pfaelzer, Jean. *Driven Out: the Forgotten War against Chinese Americans*. New York: Random House, 2007.

Shepherd, Charles R. *The Ways of Ah Sin: a Composite Narrative of Things as They Are*. New York: Fleming H. Revell, 1923.

Strobridge, Edson T. "Rev. Dr. John Todd's Dedicatory Prayer." First Transcontinental Railroad - Central Pacific Railroad Photographic History Museum. 2003.

Wilder, Laura Ingalls, and Almanzo Wilder. *West from Home: Letters of Laura Ingalls Wilder to Almanzo Wilder, San Francisco, 1915*. New York: Harper & Row, 1974.

Wilson, Carol Green. *Chinatown Quest*. California Historical, 1931.

Women's Occidental Board of Foreign Missions. Annual Report, 1874-1920. San Francisco Theological Seminary, San Anselmo, Calif.

Yep, Laurence, and Kathleen S. Yep. *The Dragon's Child: a Story of Angel Island*. New York,: HarperCollins, 2008.

Young, Robert. *The Transcontinental Railroad: America at Its Best?* Parsippany, NJ: Dillon, 1996.

Yung, Judy and the Chinese Historical Society of America. *San Francisco's Chinatown*. Charleston, South Carolina: Arcadia Publishing, 2006. Print.

Yung, Judy. *Unbound Feet: A Social History of Chinese Women in San Francisco*. Berkeley: University of California, 1995.
Yung, Judy. *Unbound Voices: a Documentary History of Chinese Women in San Francisco*. Berkeley: University of California, 1999.

Acknowledgements

This book most certainly never would have materialized from dream to reality without the gracious and dedicated support of so many wonderful people.

Thank you to the Donaldina Cameron House and everyone there who graciously welcomed two girls from the midwest. Thank you to the ECHO group for enthusiastically leading the way with book sales. Thank you, Jeanette Wei, for sharing your life and telling us about the roses. Thank you, Harry Chuck, for your openness and seasoned wisdom. Thank you, Doreen Der-McLeod, for answering countless historical questions, writing us an appendix, and telling us your story. And thank you, Laurene Chan, for your gigantic hospitality, your contagious enthusiasm, and your warm friendship.

To Bob Kwong—We are so very thankful for your generous hospitality and encouragement.

Thank you to the library of the San Francisco Theological Seminary, the castle on a hill where Kathryn lost her sweater and we almost missed the ferry. Thank you to the San Francisco City Library and Stanford University—it was thrilling to research in your collections. And thank you to the outstanding team at our very own Saline District Library who have fetched us many a book and answered many a question.

Thank you to our "couldn't have done it without you" Kickstarter supporters who sponsored the research and writing of the book. It was great fun knowing you were backing us. Particular thanks to Brett Harris; Phil and Vicky Lim; Herbert and Mary Lynne Swick; Winston Wu with the Chinese American Citizens Alliance Youth Council of Los Angeles; the anonymous Dr. & Mrs. from Charlotte, North Carolina; and the vibrant fund-raising team of Hannah Blaauw, Sarah Chen, and Clara Wong.

Thank you to those who read the manuscript in its various stages: Meg Dunn, Eleanore Keenan, Loretta Meier, Catherine Rogers,

Mary Wiland, and Wendy Wiland. Thank you to Dirk Wierenga for his experienced publishing advice and to Bill Kerschbaum of Intext Writing for editing. Our relieved thanks to Bobby Glushko from the University of Michigan copyright office for helping us cut through the Gordian knot of photo copyright law.

We are grateful to everyone who helped us with design and technical conundrums. Besides the scores of friends who got us through the little bumps along the way, we must especially thank Sarah Espinosa for her kind help with design; Ching Ru Wang, Janet Chen, Kwai Ling Ng and John Ng for expert advice on the Chinese characters; and the outstanding publicity team of Wiland & Wiland (that's Mary and Wendy). What a gift it was to see that website!

Thank you to Cheryl Corey and Stephanie Reedy from McNaughton & Gunn for your dedicated and professional assisstance. We never would have been able to navigate the many nuances of the publishing industry without your guidance.

We are thankful for the enthusiastic support of three teachers from Saline High School. Thank you, Jacqueline Majestic, for jumping on board with this crazy project. Thank you, Cristin Hodgens, for your encouragement, guidance, and support from the very beginning. And Mrs. Budnik: We'll always remember a lunchtime conversation in your classroom that ended with "You two should write this book together." This crazy idea was yours, and we are so grateful for your constant cheerleading and confidence that it really would happen.

To our community at Knox Presbyterian Church: You have been a huge part of making us who we are and of strengthening us for this project. Thanks for patiently listening to our stories of Donaldina and encouraging us to keep telling them the best that we could, and for all the help (dinner and nerf guns!) along the way. And to Reverend Chuck Jacob: Your years of sermons and friendship are surely embedded in this "Leaf by Niggle" offering.

It seems that it is always the closest family that is most inconvenienced by a book-writing venture. Thank you so very much to Phil (Dad), Clara, Ben, and Josiah, for everything. Time to have some fun.

In another generation no one will know or care who Donaldina Cameron was.
–Donaldina Cameron